TALES FROM THE

TORONTO MAPLE LEAFS

LOCKER ROOM

TALES FROM THE

TORONTO MAPLE LEAFS

LOCKER ROOM

A COLLECTION OF THE GREATEST
MAPLE LEAFS STORIES EVER TOLD

DAVID SHOALTS

SPORTS
PUBLISHING

Sports Publishing books may be purchased in bulk at special discounts for
sales promotion, corporate gifts, fund-raising, or educational purposes. Special
editions can also be created to specifications. For details, contact the Special
Sales Department, Sports Publishing, 307 West 36th Street, 11th Floor, New
York, NY 10018 or sportspubbooks@skyhorsepublishing.com.

Sports Publishing® is a registered trademark of Skyhorse Publishing, Inc.®, a
Delaware corporation.

Visit our website at www.sportspubbooks.com.

10 9 8 7 6 5 4 3 2 1

Library of Congress Cataloging-in-Publication Data is available on file.

ISBN: 978-1-61321-240-0

Printed in the United States of America

To Yvonne, Rebecca, and Matthew

CONTENTS

ACKNOWLEDGMENTS

When a team has a history as long and rich (at least in the earlier years) as the Toronto Maple Leafs, many of its stories pass into legend. Leaf fans of a certain age are all familiar with them, from how Conn Smythe got Maple Leaf Gardens built by convincing the workers to accept Gardens shares as part of their salaries, to the triumph of Bobby Baun's game-winning goal in overtime in the Stanley Cup final on a broken leg, to the time Darryl Sittler ripped the captain's C off his sweater in protest of the trade of a friend.

The purpose of this book is not to retell all of those old stories, although the Baun saga is found here. Nor is this an anecdotal history of the franchise. This is a collection of stories that some people connected to the Leafs tell over dinner or a few drinks, tales that are interesting or funny or both. There is no historical thread here, only a wish to entertain.

I am indebted to a large group of people for these stories, some of whom wish to remain anonymous, given the nature of their anecdotes. My thanks go to all of them.

Bob Haggert, who was hired by Conn Smythe and Hap Day in the 1950s as a trainer and served through the first Punch Imlach era, was especially generous with his time. So was Jim McKenny, who played for Imlach and a succession of coaches through the 1970s and then took his talent for talk to television.

The Stellick brothers, Gord and Bob, are a couple of Toronto boys who landed dream jobs while they were still in high school—go-fers for the Maple Leafs. Both parlayed their jobs into long careers with the Leafs, with Gord rising to general manager and Bob to public relations director. They were witness to a lot of wild and wonderful events along the way, and I thank both men for sharing them.

Also generous with their time and recollections were a group of former and current Leaf staffers and players who are now, like Gord Stellick and McKenny, in the broadcasting business. Bill Watters, the former assistant GM of the Leafs, and his old sidekick Joe Bowen, the sworn enemy of silence who still calls Leaf games, were invaluable. Glenn Healy, contender for the title of the world's most loquacious goalie, and Bob McGill also contributed.

There were many reference materials I consulted to check factual matters such as times, dates, and names. The one I found myself picking up more than any other was Toronto author Jack Batten's anecdotal history, *The Leafs.*

My fellow hockey writers in Toronto were also a valuable resource, particularly Lance Hornby of the *Toronto Sun* and Paul Hunter of the *Toronto Star.* I would especially like to thank my friend and colleague at *The Globe and Mail,* Tim Wharnsby. My boss, *Globe* sports editor Steve McAllister, also deserves a salute for his support.

Finally, books do not get written while holding down a full-time job unless you have a supportive family. This is the second book I've written, and like the first one, it came along in the midst of a major home renovation project. I am forever grateful to my wife, Yvonne, who said, "Just worry about the book," and to my children, Rebecca and Matthew, for their support. I also owe many thanks to my father, Roy, for his leadership on the renovation side and to my mother, Vivian, for not minding all the time Dad spends on it.

1

LEAFS POTPOURRI

Walter Gretzky, hockey's most famous dad, is also one of the world's most famous Toronto Maple Leafs fans. This is not an act of disloyalty to his son Wayne, who came close on one occasion but never did play for the Maple Leafs. As a native of Brantford, Ontario, just a 90-minute drive from Toronto, it is natural for Walter to cheer for the Blue and White, and he is a fixture at the Air Canada Centre.

In the summer of 2005, Wayne decided to reward his father's loyalty by purchasing a road trip with the Maple Leafs for him at a charity auction. As it turned out, the trip in early January 2006 was therapeutic for Walter. It came a couple of weeks after his wife and Wayne's mother, Phyllis, had died of cancer.

Walter got to travel on the Leafs' charter flights, stay at their hotel, and ride on the team bus. He told reporters the trip helped him cope with the loss of his wife.

However, the trip did not start well for the diehard Leafs fan. The Leafs lost their first game 1–0 to the Calgary Flames, and all agreed they did not play well. Naturally Walter was not happy, although he is not the kind of fellow to throw a public tantrum.

The next night they were in Edmonton, and a few hours before the game Walter and the Leafs climbed on the team bus for the ride from the hotel to the arena. As soon as the bus was underway, Walter stood up, went to the back of the bus, and faced the players.

"Well, ladies, are we going to be better tonight?" he asked.

The Leafs responded with a 3–2 win over the Oilers, and Walter was smiling again.

In the years after the Air Canada Centre opened on February 20, 1999, the tour guides had a favourite story about the Maple Leafs dressing room that involved head coach Pat Quinn and the Leaf logo on the floor.

Before I tell the tale, there are a couple of things to remember about Quinn in those days. One, Quinn's relationship with his players did not lend itself to heartfelt, emotional speeches. Two, before a heart arrhythmia frightened the coach into embracing a healthier lifestyle, Quinn's love of cigars, good scotch, and thick steaks, along with a hip replacement, kept him well north of the slim line.

Now, as is the fashion in many NHL cities, the Leaf logo is emblazoned on the carpet in the middle of the dressing room. Some teams have functionaries shooing interlopers from their logo, telling them not to step on it. The Leafs, however, very sensibly keep theirs covered up by a circular rug. This is where the tour guide's tale comes in.

At least one tour guide was said to regularly take a group of wide-eyed fans into the Leaf dressing room and gather them around the Leaf logo. "Before every Leaf game," the guide would say, "Pat Quinn gives his pep talk to the players. Then, as he finishes, Mr. Quinn bends over, pulls the rug off the logo, and yells, 'Go get 'em, boys!' Then the players charge out to the ice."

This apocryphal tale was related to a member of the Leafs staff who worked with the players. He considered the corpulent, slow-moving coach and said, "It would be news if Quinn bent over for anything."

Floyd Smith was in the employ of the Maple Leafs for many years, starting in the late 1960s. He served the Leafs as a player, scout, and from

1989 to 1991, as general manager. He was not known for his sense of humour, but he was famous among those around the Leafs as one of the most unintentionally funny men in hockey.

This became clear early in his tenure as GM when a group of reporters collared him for comment about the future of head coach Doug Carpenter, whose job was said to be in jeopardy. Smith raised his hands and said to the approaching group, "Fellas, I've got nothing to say, and I'm only going to say it once."

Tim Wharnsby, my fellow hockey writer at *The Globe and Mail,* loves to tell this story about Smith. Tim was working for *The Toronto Sun* at the time, a young fellow in his first year on the Leaf beat, trying not to let all of the big-leaguers completely intimidate him.

This time, it was Smith's job security that was the subject of speculation. Jim O'Leary and Mike Simpson ran the *Sun* sports section at the time, and they wanted Smith's opinion of the rumours that Cliff Fletcher was about to take his job as general manager. Wharnsby was in Quebec with the Leafs for a game against the Nordiques. He was told to ask Smith about the situation.

Wharnsby went up to Smith at Le Colisée, the Nordiques arena, and steeled himself for the difficult question.

"Mr. Smith, my bosses told me to ask you if you were going to be fired," Wharnsby said, fighting the urge to run away.

"Tell me, Timmy, who are your bosses?"

"Jim O'Leary and Mike Simpson."

"Well, Timmy, you tell Jim O'Leary and Mike Simpson to go fuck themselves."

Another longtime Leaf retainer with a funny streak is George Armstrong, whose tenure started in 1949 as a player at the age of 19 when he came to Toronto from Northern Ontario. Armstrong has been a player and a coach during his seven decades with the Leafs and remains with the team today as a scout. Unlike Smith, however, there was never anything unintentional about his humour.

Armstrong reluctantly allowed himself to be pressed into service as head coach 33 games into the 1988-89 season when John Brophy was fired. In the summer of 1989, GM Floyd Smith relieved Armstrong of a job he never wanted and hired Doug Carpenter as head coach. Word went around that Carpenter and Armstrong were distant relatives.

Tim Wharnsby asked Armstrong if this were true.

"Yes," Armstrong said.

"How are you related?"

"Well, Timmy," Armstrong replied, "A long time ago, one of my relatives fucked one of his relatives."

Mats Sundin is known as one of the most affable players to ever wear a Leaf uniform. While he is not a colourful speaker, Sundin usually shoulders his media duties with patience and rarely takes issue with his interrogators.

The one exception, though, is when reporters want to look into his private life. Sundin is an intensely private person who rarely discusses his family and never discusses his love life. It was the topic of his love life that drove Sundin to drop an f-bomb in front of the media for the first time since he became a Maple Leaf in 1994.

It happened on March 29, 2000, when the Leafs were in St. Louis to play the Blues. Mike Kitchen, then an assistant coach with the Blues, started his coaching career with the Leafs and knew Mats well. Kitchen dropped by the Toronto practice at the Blues' rink to tease his old friend.

Kitchen walked to the Leafs' bench as they were on the ice and called out to Sundin in the presence of the beat reporters covering the team. He said a former Leaf, Fredrik Modin, told him Sundin was getting married to Tina Fagerstrom, then his longtime girlfriend. Sundin immediately declared it was not true.

It was clear Kitchen was merely joking, so none of the reporters were serious when the topic was brought up after practice with Sundin. "There's nothing to that," he said.

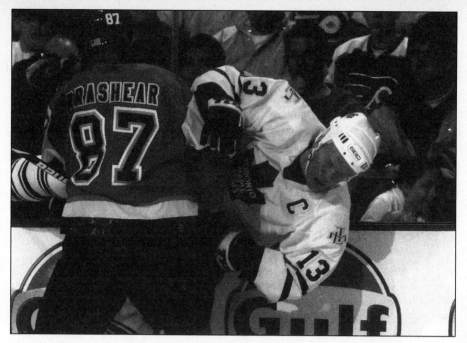

Mats Sundin rarely used the f-word off the ice but may have here when Donald Brashear of the Philadelphia Flyers drove him into the boards.

No one planned to write anything about it until a radio reporter decided it was worth stop-the-presses treatment on his noon-hour report just after the Leaf practice ended. This meant the print reporters had to cover themselves with their bosses, so we all filed a short item about the story and explained it was merely Kitchen teasing his old friend.

But Sundin did not see anything funny about the items. He was still steaming the next day when the reporters showed up at the Leafs' game-day skate.

"You fuckers," he snapped at the group.

That really raised the eyebrows of the assembled scribes, who had never heard Sundin utter an angry word let alone a profane one.

Before Sundin's long run as the resident Leafs hero, Doug Gilmour carried that mantle in the mid-1990s. Gilmour arrived in the biggest trade in Leafs history, one that involved 10 players on January 2, 1992. And he left on February 25, 1997, when he was traded to the New Jersey Devils.

Rumours circulated before the Devils trade that Gilmour wanted out, but things were not that simple. Gilmour's exodus began when the hockey season ended in 1996 and he and general manager Cliff Fletcher sat down to talk about a new contract. Fletcher offered Gilmour what's known in the NHL as a retirement contract. It was for several years at a salary that may have seemed high in relation to his scoring totals but which recognized his past contributions to the team. Once the contract was up, the intimation was that Gilmour would retire and take a position in the front office.

The problem was, Gilmour was not sure exactly when he wanted to retire. He was also not comfortable with the idea of getting paid far more than his current worth in the last year or two of the contract.

"There were a lot of stories circulated that I wanted out," Gilmour said. "I'm not going to get into details, but I was offered some money to kind of retire [in Toronto] by the team. I was not prepared to do it at the time."

Gilmour wrestled with the idea for a few weeks, talking it over with his wife, Amy.

"The contract gave me security, but at the same time," Gilmour asked himself, "Do I want to continue playing? I can look back at my career and say a lot of it I did it my way. I was not looking to hang on just because I was in Toronto."

Finally, he decided to accept the deal.

"As we got closer to it, I said to Cliff, 'Maybe I will accept that deal,'" Gilmour said. "But he said it was not on the table any more. They took it off the table. It wasn't Cliff, it was upper management. That's how it came down."

Steve Stavro, the chairman of the board of directors of what is now called Maple Leaf Sports and Entertainment, and his fellow directors decreed the team had to cut costs. Also shipped out that summer were expensive veterans Mike Gartner and Dave Gagner. Earlier, Todd Gill and Dave Andreychuk, a 50-goal scorer, were dumped. Gilmour said he knew then his days as a Leaf were numbered, although he did not demand a trade.

"I accepted it," he said. "It's time to go when upper management doesn't want you. It doesn't matter what business you're in—if you have an investment, and you think that investment is going down, and you have a chance to bring in new players or new workers, you do it.

"I have no bitter feelings about it at all, that's just how it works. I said at the time I'm not going to cry over it, I'll go somewhere else. But it was kind of disappointing how it turned out."

A few weeks before the trading deadline, on February 25, 1997, Gilmour, defenceman Dave Ellett, and a third-round pick in the 1999 NHL Entry Draft were traded to the New Jersey Devils for defenceman Jason Smith and forwards Alyn McCauley and Steve Sullivan.

The austerity kick cost the Maple Leafs a lot more than Gilmour in the summer of 1996. It also cost them the chance of having Gilmour, Sundin, and Wayne Gretzky as their top three centres.

For a few weeks in June 1996, the same time as he was trying to negotiate a contract with Gilmour, Fletcher thought he was going to land Gretzky as a free agent.

Gretzky's representatives contacted Fletcher. Gretzky was an unrestricted free agent and had no interest in signing a new contract with the St. Louis Blues, who picked him up in a trade with the Los Angeles Kings during the 1995-96 season. Gretzky grew up as a Maple Leaf fan in Brantford, Ontario, and at the age of 35, he wanted to finish his career with the Leafs.

Fletcher was told Gretzky was so eager to do this, he was willing to turn down an offer of $8 million a year from the Vancouver Canucks and sign with the Leafs for between $2 million and $3 million. The deal was that in a major media and business centre like Toronto, Gretzky and the Leafs would make up the difference with endorsement and sponsorship money.

The Leafs GM decided to run the idea past his captain.

"Yeah, Cliff called me into his office," Gilmour said. "I said, 'What have I done now?' He said, 'No, no, we have opportunity to get Wayne here. What do you think?' I said, 'Go for it.'"

Gilmour even offered to give up his captain's title to Gretzky, but Fletcher said that would not be necessary. "We'll make him an assistant captain," Fletcher said.

"'I really don't care about that. Just get him here to help us win,'" Gilmour said. "I don't know the details of what happened. I just know something happened with Stavro."

Stavro and the other Maple Leaf Gardens directors stepped in and nixed the deal. Gretzky said later he was told the Gardens directors slashed the payroll to direct as much money as possible toward building the Air Canada Centre, which opened in February 1999. Around the same time, Stavro had to cough up more than $20 million to settle a nasty lawsuit over the value of the Gardens stock when he wrested control of the company from Harold Ballard's estate.

Gretzky wound up signing with the New York Rangers. The Leafs missed the 1997 playoffs, and Fletcher soon joined Gilmour in exile.

If Fletcher had managed to sign Gretzky, there would have been even more material for the newspapers than might be expected. Three years earlier, Gretzky played a starring role in breaking the hearts of the Leafs and their fans, who were hoping the team would make the Stanley Cup Final for the first time since 1967.

The details are seared into the brains of every Leaf fan of a certain age. The Leafs held a 3–2 lead over the Kings in the best-of-seven Campbell Conference final in 1993 when they went into Los Angeles for Game 6 on May 27.

Down 4–2 with nine minutes left in the third period, the Leafs stormed back to send the game into overtime. When overtime started, though, the Kings were on the power play because Leaf winger Glenn Anderson was given a penalty with 13 seconds left in the third period.

Then, 39 seconds into overtime, Gretzky clipped Gilmour on the face with his stick, leaving a cut severe enough to require eight stitches. Referee Kerry Fraser, who was involved in several Leaf controversies over the years, did not see the infraction. Neither did the two linesmen. Shortly after that, Gretzky scored the winning goal to tie the series. Back in Toronto for Game 7, Gretzky drove a dagger into the Leafs' hearts with one of his greatest games ever, scoring three goals in a 5–4 Kings victory that ended the series.

"If Kerry Fraser hadn't seen the call, which obviously he didn't as he says, the linesmen should have made the call," Gilmour said. "Give him two minutes. With Glenn Anderson in the box already, it would have just evened out. It's sad and disappointing that three people on the ice did not see it, especially when it happened at a face-off."

To this day, Gilmour believes Gretzky and Kings had more than their share of luck in that series. This despite the fact the Leafs went into the series as the Cinderella team, having knocked off the heavily favoured Detroit Red Wings in the first round of the playoffs.

"If you told anybody in this league, give me the seventh game of the semifinals at home, would you take it?" Gilmour asked. "Damn right I would. Unfortunately, Gretzky had one of his career games and beat us. We gave it a good run.

"You could say we had a horseshoe somewhere, but look at some of the goals [the Kings] scored. They got some lucky goals. We made some mistakes that we really didn't make that often."

The Leafs came back from the loss in the Stanley Cup semifinals in 1993 to make the NHL's Final Four again in 1994. They were not as strong this time, in large part because their heart and soul, Gilmour, had to cope with a foot injury he had suffered in the first round against the Chicago Blackhawks. He carried the Leafs to a win over Chicago in six games by having his ankle frozen for the last few games. Gilmour said his foot got better in the next round against the San Jose Sharks, but the Leafs ran out of gas in the semifinals and lost to the Vancouver

Canucks in five games.

By then, Gilmour could go no further. Between his injury and the 30 or more minutes of icetime in each playoff game, Gilmour became increasingly haggard. At the end, his drawn features and sunken eyes gave him the look of a famine victim.

"I had a bone chip in my ankle against Chicago, and that was a lot of pain," Gilmour said. "There's no way I could have played that sixth game if there hadn't been a couple of needles. At the morning skate [for Game 6], I went out, but I couldn't skate on it. I went out in the warm-up for the game and still couldn't skate, so my foot was frozen.

"The hardest thing when they freeze your foot is you don't know how tight your skate is. And when you go to kick the puck, you might miss it. It's a really weird feeling. I had to watch it but the doctors said I wouldn't have any repercussions from it. By the San Jose series, I was down to one needle a game, and against Vancouver the needles were done. I was down to Tylenol."

After the Leafs traded him, Gilmour played five and a half more seasons with the New Jersey Devils, Chicago Blackhawks, Buffalo Sabres, and Montreal Canadiens. On March 11, 2003, Gilmour came back to the Leafs in a trade with the Canadiens to bolster them for the playoff run. But in his first game, Gilmour suffered a serious knee injury and his season was over. Gilmour tried to rehabilitate his knee, but progress was slow. With no guarantee the Leafs would welcome him back even if he recovered, Gilmour announced his retirement in September 2003 at the age of 39 after 20 seasons in the NHL.

There were some hard feelings at the time between Gilmour and the Leafs' rookie general manager, John Ferguson. At his first press conference, Ferguson was asked if Gilmour had a place on the team, and he essentially said no. Most GMs in that position would have done some tap dancing, considering Gilmour's place in the affections of Leaf fans, saying something to the effect of "We'll take a look at him if his rehabilitation goes well." But Ferguson was new to dealing with the

Toronto media, and shortly afterward, Gilmour made his announcement.

"I was trying to get my leg back to where I wanted it to be and possibly have one more chance to play," Gilmour said. "Some comments were made, and at that time I made my decision to retire. It was not worth it to try and play in another city."

Actually, Gilmour said, he and Ferguson made their peace shortly after the GM's misstep.

"I had a good chat with John," Gilmour said. "He said it came out wrong and I made a mistake in how I said it. He said, 'Continue your workouts, and if you feel you want to come back, give us a call.'

"But at that time, I was a player who had played 20 years. With the injury I had, I had to wonder if it was worth pushing it that much with my future in limbo. So I made my decision. I knew I could go somewhere else and play, but I didn't want to move my family, so I just shut it down."

Three years later, on September 15, 2006, Gilmour joined the Leafs front office as their professional development advisor. His duties include scouting and giving advice to younger players at all levels of the Leafs system.

After he retired, Gilmour was still visible around the team. He hung on to the season tickets he bought in his first stint with the Leafs and stayed in touch with his former teammates. He also coached his two sons, Jake and Tyson.

Jake was eight years old when Gilmour retired and Tyson was six, and it just happened to be the year they grew passionate about the Leafs. Gilmour was at the Air Canada Centre with them one day when they ran into Leafs head coach Pat Quinn.

"I took them down to a practice on a Saturday shortly after I retired," Gilmour said. "It was a game day, and I had to pick up some sticks and clear out my spot in the dressing room. It might have been the fourth or fifth game into the season.

"Kids can get a little spoiled about going to the rink all the time. They don't understand from their side that when my job was done they didn't get carte blanche to go down to the Air Canada Centre any more.

"Pat Quinn was walking out to go to practice when Jake saw him. He said, very innocently, 'How come my dad can't skate down here anymore?'

"Mr. Quinn said to him, 'Listen son, your dad can skate down here any time he wants.'

"So Jake said, 'Dad, get your skates, we can still go.' I had to say, 'No, Jake, it doesn't work that way.'"

During the NHL lockout in the 1994-95 season, Gilmour decided to play in Switzerland to keep himself in playing shape. He signed on with SC Rapperswil-Jona in the Swiss league and set out for the small town of Rapperswil, near Zurich, with a group of reporters, photographers, and his agent, Larry Kelly, in tow.

According to one of the reporters, Lance Hornby of the *Toronto Sun,* Gilmour was kept on the go for 36 consecutive hours, starting with his flight from Toronto to Zurich. The small party left Toronto at 7 p.m. and arrived in Zurich at 4 a.m. Toronto time.

The owner of the Swiss team held a reception at the airport for Gilmour, which included a press conference for the local media. Then Gilmour was taken on a 30-minute drive to Rapperswil and his first practice with his new team at noon. Right after practice, Gilmour went for lunch with his new teammates and then to another press conference, this one for the Swiss national media. Gilmour then got a couple of hours of sleep in a chair at his hotel before a second practice with his team at 7:15 p.m., local time, followed by a video session.

Once his obligations were finally over, Gilmour headed back to his hotel, where someone in the party (Hornby insists it wasn't him) suggested a drink in the bar. Gilmour, ever the trooper, joined the group, and Hornby says they discovered the bar had a jukebox with '60s and '70s tunes. A name-that-tune contest sprang up, but jet lag finally caught up to Gilmour and he nodded off at the bar.

At one point, the song "Little Arrows" came on and no one could come up with the person who sang it. Suddenly, Gilmour's head snapped up. He raised his hand and said, "Leapy Lee," the correct answer, and then his head hit the bar again.

At the big press conference after Gilmour's arrival in Rapperswil, Hornby found himself on the wrong end of a misunderstanding caused by one local reporter's shaky grasp of English.

The sweaters players wear in the Swiss league are covered in logos for all manner of sponsors to the point where the team colours are barely visible. Like all of the other new arrivals, Hornby was curious about the sweaters.

One of the local Swiss reporters was a friendly fellow who was helpful when Hornby first arrived, so he asked the man if some of the team's sweaters would be at the press conference. The man assured him they would.

A few minutes later, a large woman, obviously a fan, came into the room wearing a hockey sweater covered in logos. Hornby turned to the local reporter, pointed at the woman and asked, "Is this the hockey sweater?" The previously friendly fellow instantly grew enraged. "Zis iss no hockey player!" he shouted. "Zis iss my vife!"

Pat Burns was one of the most colourful characters to serve as head coach of the Leafs. With his dark brown pompadour, fiery temper, and stinging wit, the former cop commanded a lot of attention as well as respect.

At the start of the 1994-95 season, Burns' second behind the Leafs bench, the team bolted to a 10-0 start, an NHL record. Once the Leafs hit five wins, the streak and the possibility of setting a new NHL record became a big topic for the Toronto media. The pressure on the players

grew and, as he recalled on Bill Watters' radio show, Burns realized it when he decided his No. 1 goaltender, Felix Potvin, needed a rest.

Around the sixth game, Burns approached Damian Rhodes, the backup, about making a start in goal.

"I didn't want to play Felix Potvin that many games in a row," Burns said. "I wanted to give him a break. But Rhodes said, 'I don't want to go in there.' I don't think he wanted to be the guy who lost and stopped the streak.

"I said, 'You better go in there.'"

Rhodes knew better than to argue. He started the next game, the Leafs won, and the streak continued.

Paul Maurice, who succeeded Pat Quinn as head coach in 2006, is another fellow known to put on his interviewers. Early in Maurice's first season as coach, the prime minister of Canada, Stephen Harper, who happens to be a big Leaf fan and a hockey historian as well, attended a game at the Air Canada Centre. Maurice was on television before the game, and he was asked if he knew who Stephen Harper was.

"Yeah, he's the owner of the Harp Brewery," Maurice said. There was a long pause. It was filled with the laughter of the cameramen, who knew their beverages and got the joke.

After the game, though, Maurice discovered at least one viewer did not think he was too funny.

"The camera men must be drinkers, because they got the joke," he said. "But my mom was mad when she called me on the cell after the game and said, 'You don't know who the prime minister is?'"

Prime Minister Harper paid a visit to the Leafs dressing room after the same game, a 4–1 loss to the Ottawa Senators. Not all of the Leafs felt like schmoozing.

Doug Gilmour missed a chance to play with Mats Sundin and Wayne Gretzky because of an austerity kick by senior management.

"I just said, 'Very nice to meet you,'" forward Darcy Tucker said. "We'd just lost, so there wasn't a lot to say."

But Wade Belak, whose carefree disposition belies his role as the team enforcer, thought he should put his brief face time with the PM to good use.

"I asked him if he could do something to get me in a lower tax bracket," Belak said. "I've now met the prime minister and the Trailer Park Boys [during an exhibition stop in Halifax]. It's been a pretty good month."

Another Leaf coach who had a good sense of humour was John Brophy. He also had a volcanic temper, however, which was unleashed more often than not by his inept Leaf teams in the late 1980s.

But early in the 1986-87 season, Lance Hornby recalls, Brophy was often in a good mood because the team got off to a great start. On one road trip to St. Louis, Brophy was downright giddy, much to the chagrin of assistant coach Garry Lariviere.

The Leafs arrived in St. Louis the day before the game, and the Blues happened to be playing another NHL team that night at the old Arena. Lariviere suggested they go to the game to scout the Blues, but Brophy, happy with his team's hot start, wasn't interested. Lariviere insisted, and Brophy finally, grudgingly agreed to go to the game. Before he left, the coach told Hornby and a couple of other writers that he and Lariviere would meet them after the game for a drink.

When Brophy and Lariviere arrived at the bar, which was just up the street from the team hotel, Lariviere was sporting a cut on his head that was quite noticeable given his sparse crop of hair. The pair told the writers the cut was the result of some horseplay in the press box.

"Lariviere was trying to write the Blues' line combinations down, but Brophy kept hitting him with his shoulder," Hornby said. "At one point, he bumped him so hard that Lariviere dropped his pen. He bent over to get it, and Brophy playfully punched him in the head. But he had a large ring from one of his minor-league championships on that hand,

Leafs head coach Paul Maurice drew the wrath of his mother with a quip about Canada's prime minister.

and it cut Lariviere's head."

Lariviere insisted on staying until the end of the game, though, holding a napkin on the cut.

Brophy's good humour was tested shortly after the previous story was recounted to the Toronto hockey writers. The group left the bar and returned to the team hotel just as a tiny sports car pulled up to the curb.

Brophy and Lariviere noticed the car was packed full of people and laughed when one of its doors flew open and a couple of gorgeous women spilled out. But they stopped laughing when the next two people out of the car were a Leaf rookie, who was the team's hottest scorer at the time, and a married veteran. Nonetheless, the Leafs were playing well enough that Brophy didn't stop the two players as they sashayed into the hotel with their guests.

The next night, the Leafs lost, starting a long slide in the standings, and the rookie failed to score. In fact, Hornby said, it was a long time before the rookie scored again, at least on the ice.

In those years, the Leafs developed a fierce rivalry with the Blues, in part because the teams met a couple of times in the playoffs and in part because the Blues GM in those days, Ron Caron, could get just as fiery as Brophy. Caron's antics in the press box during games were legendary. He would get so worked up at what was happening on the ice he could be heard all over the arena. On one occasion at Maple Leaf Gardens, when Leafs public relations man Bob Stellick tried to get him to tone it down, Caron threw a chair at him and challenged him to a fight.

In the spring of 1987, the Blues and Leafs met in the playoffs, and it wasn't long before Caron and Brophy were trading shots through the media. This skirmish was started when Caron and his head coach, Jacques Martin, complained the Leafs were getting away with all manner of hooking and holding. Brophy fired back when he was asked about his plan for the next game in the series.

"We're going to slash and hack and do all of that stuff Ronnie Caron doesn't like," Brophy said. "It'll be old-time hockey."

"Who do they think they're playing, an old bag of rags? You'd think they'd been Stanley Cup champions for the last 15 years."

One of the worst lows for Brophy as the Leafs coach came on February 22, 1988, after a game in Minnesota against the North Stars. The North Stars were one of the very few teams in the NHL worse than the Leafs at that point, but thanks to the league's playoff system, both teams had a chance for the last playoff spot in the Norris Division.

Thus, every game that season against the North Stars was important. But the Leafs, after a promising start to the road trip, went into Minnesota, rolled over, and died. By the end of the 4–2 loss, Brophy was fed up. His players could not muster a decent effort against a woeful team and finished an important western road trip with a 1-2-1 record.

The coach's frustrations boiled over in his postgame interview with reporters Lance Hornby of the *Toronto Sun* and Mark Harding of the *Toronto Star*. Brophy let it all out, calling his players a disgrace to the Leaf uniform. He also said there was no hope of turning things around because everyone in the league knew his players were terrible and had no interest in trading for any of them. When the reporters gathered around him outside the Leaf dressing room, Brophy started slowly. But he soon warmed to the topic, increasing his intensity and the volume.

It was a spectacular, profane, volcanic rant, and Hornby captured it all on his microcassette recorder.

"I had a goaltender working tonight, Todd Gill on defence and Rick Lanz working tonight and [Greg] Terrion and Peter Ihnacak and [Mike] Blaisdell were the only guys who worked on this hockey club tonight," Brophy said, and then practically spat out the next sentence: "The rest of them stunk the fucking joint out."

Then the coach's voice grew in volume.

"I got to fucking seriously consider what the fuck we got on this hockey club," he said. "They're not fucking fooling nobody, most of all they're not fooling anybody else in the fucking league, I'll tell you that.

"I'm sick and fucking tired of making excuses. And all these fucking guys that are getting paid on this fucking hockey club blame it on someone else all the fucking time."

At this point, Hornby asked if any changes to the lineup were being considered.

"Make changes?" Brophy said incredulously. "Why do you think we play like that for Christ's sake? You think the door is being knocked down [with offers] for our players?

"Embarrassing? It's fucking embarrassing without fucking question. It's embarrassing, embarrassing, embarrassing, without that it's very fucking embarrassing. But it's never around who the fuck is playing the games. It's always embarrassing for somebody else."

At this point, Brophy wound down and told the reporters to go in the dressing room and try to get some answers from the players. But a few minutes later, assistant coach Garry Lariviere went into the room and summoned the reporters outside once more. Brophy had more to say, he said. The coach then clicked into overdrive, giving the f-word a workout in all of its forms.

In the second session, Brophy went from rage to bewilderment to rage to despair and, finally, to weary resignation. He also set what is believed to be a modern NHL record for use of the f-bomb and its variations in a postgame interview—72 (Hornby counted).

Brophy was a man who spent his entire playing career in the low minor leagues and almost all of his coaching career there as well. He was a hard man who grew up in a hard place and in hard times, during the Depression in rural Nova Scotia. The attitude of the pampered modern athlete was something he could never understand, and it came through loud and clear as he unburdened himself to the Toronto hockey writers. Brophy's voice rose to a combination of rage and bewilderment in Part II.

"Who are those fucking guys anyway? Who the fuck do they think they are?" he asked. "And who the fuck do they think they're kidding? Where do they get the nuts to come to the fucking rink every second day and fourth day and play one period a week and get away with it?"

The climax came when he, a man who thought anyone should be proud to wear the Maple Leaf, wondered about his players' lack of pride: "Who are these fucking people that drag that uniform through the mud for Christ's sake? There's been great players play in the thing, and they act like this here. Who are they?"

There was worse to come. The Leafs finished the 1987-88 season with a 21-49-10 record but still made the playoffs. They lost in the first round to the Detroit Red Wings.

That series was notable as the lowest point in franchise history. The Red Wings humiliated the Leafs 8–0 at Maple Leaf Gardens in Game 4 of the series to take a 3-1 lead. As they had done so often in the regular season, the players quit once the Red Wings opened up a 3–0 lead.

But on this night, the regular, complacent corporate crowd was not in the stands. The toffs had either sold or given away their playoff tickets, so the stands were full of ordinary fans. And they had had a bellyful of their heroes.

When one angry fan took off his Leaf sweater, tied it in a knot, and threw it from the end blues to the ice, it set off a torrent of rage. Debris and verbal abuse showered down from the seats, and the game had to be stopped. This continued off and on for the rest of the game.

Change for the better was still a long way away. Brophy held on to his job, but by Christmas of 1988 in the following season, he was gone, fired by new GM Gord Stellick. The Leafs missed the playoffs altogether in the 1988-89 season.

As with any major sports beat, many of the reporters covering the Maple Leafs over the years used their wit and the pages of their newspapers to skewer the more disagreeable people running the team. This also involved methods far more subtle than the usual rip job on a GM or coach whose team was not winning.

Don Ramsay covered the Leafs for many years for *The Globe and Mail.* His career ended badly after he moved to the *Toronto Sun* to be a news reporter and was caught in a libel scandal. But in his younger years, he was known as an aggressive and combative reporter.

During one season on the Leaf beat, Ramsay found out a Leaf executive had a mistress. He also discovered the philandering fellow had his mistress installed in an apartment. Even Ramsay knew he could not print this information without involving his newspaper in a messy lawsuit, but he hit upon another way to skewer the fellow, with whom he had a fractious relationship.

One Saturday, near the bottom of a notebook column and stuck in the middle of several short items separated by the classic three dots was this sentence: "The most intriguing new name on the Leafs beat this season is ___," and there Ramsay printed the name of the mistress.

The executive in question flipped out, but he knew he could not make his displeasure public. So he fumed in private, and his relationship with Ramsay grew much, much colder.

One of the wittiest men to cover the Leafs was the late Rex MacLeod, who did the job for *The Globe and Mail* and the *Toronto Star* from the 1950s to the 1980s. He was famous for deflating Leaf management types from Harold Ballard to Punch Imlach with his prose.

Imlach never hesitated to tell reporters just how smart he was at running hockey teams. During his first run with the Leafs in the 1960s, Imlach had a gall bladder operation. Stories about it appeared in all of the papers. However, MacLeod's account noted the surgeon removed Imlach's bladder but left the gall.

Years later, Ballard was known to have his fading locks touched up by a hairdresser. Everyone always knew when Ballard had been in for a rinse because his hair was an odd shade of orange.

In the late 1980s, the Leafs were involved in a playoff series with the St. Louis Blues. They were the underdogs and one of the players hit upon the idea of bleaching a patch of his hair for luck. He also convinced most of his teammates to do the same.

When the team arrived at the Arena in St. Louis, their hairstyles were of great interest to the newspaper photographers standing in the concourse. Ballard came in right behind the players, and he was sporting a fresh touch-up in the familiar hue.

As the photographers snapped away, MacLeod asked loudly, "Whose dye job are you getting? Theirs or Harold's?"

MacLeod's most famous shot was in Ballard's obituary. When famous people get on in years, newspapers customarily prepare their obituaries so they will not be scrambling when the person in question passes on. MacLeod was told by his boss at the *Star* to write one for Ballard, whose health was an issue for the last 10 years of his life.

MacLeod turned in the standard treatment on Ballard, save for the last line. It read, "He was predeceased by his hockey team."

This quickly became a legend among the media types. Naturally, the line never appeared in Ballard's obituary when it ran after his death in 1990, but it did appear in MacLeod's obituary several years later.

Punch Imlach may have been the target of humour. He was never the source. Just ask Johnny Bower, the beloved Leaf goalie of the 1960s Stanley Cup winners. Bower shared the goaltending duties with Terry Sawchuk on the 1967 Leafs, the last team to bring the Stanley Cup to Toronto.

The championship is considered one of the great upsets in hockey since the Maple Leafs were an elderly team that finished a distant third in the regular season to the Chicago Blackhawks. But the Leafs knocked off the Blackhawks in the semifinals and then beat the Montreal Canadiens in the final, thanks to the work of Bower and Sawchuk, although both men would have preferred not to share the job.

During that semifinal series, Bower did not get a start until the fifth game. In the first period, he had to reach quickly for one of Bobby Hull's fearsome shots and felt a twitch in his groin.

"After a while, Punch called a timeout and sent George Armstrong to talk to me," Bower recalls. "George says, 'Punch says you're not moving. You're lateral movement is no good.'

"I said, 'George, don't say nothing, but I pulled my groin a wee bit.' I didn't want to come out because I knew it would be tough to get back in. But George says, 'He saw you. Punch can see, you know.'

"I said, 'Yeah, I know, but just go tell him I'm okay.' George went back to Punch and says, 'Bower says he's okay.'

"Then I see the Chief coming back, and he says, 'Punch says if you don't come out, he'll fine you 25 dollars.' So I had to come out. Twenty-five dollars was a lot of money for me at that time."

Bower managed to get back in goal for the second game of the final against the Montreal Canadiens and beat them. Sawchuk rightly figured that meant Bower would start again in the third game.

Sawchuk was a taciturn man who liked to take a drink. Leafs legend says that Sawchuk went on a memorable toot the night before Game 3 since he thought he was not going to play. He was right, but Bower got hurt in the pregame warm-up.

Sawchuk was said to be so hungover he could barely focus, and the Canadiens whipped him and the Leafs 6–2. Bower demurred when asked if the story were true.

"Oh, I couldn't comment on that," he said with a smile.

Nevertheless, Sawchuk stayed away from booze for the rest of the series and was the star of the Leafs' upset.

Glenn Anderson was a 50-goal scorer on the great Edmonton Oilers teams of the 1980s. Those days were well behind him when GM Cliff Fletcher landed him in a trade with the Oilers that included goaltender Grant Fuhr.

Most reporters found Anderson to be difficult, a man whose sense of humour appeared to be one long private joke. Once, no matter what question was posed by a couple of reporters, Anderson's only answer was "sex on the beach."

However, Paul Hunter of the *Toronto Star* managed to laugh after one exchange with Anderson. It came on December 30, 1991, when the Leafs were at Le Colisée in Quebec, preparing to play the speedy Nordiques. Cliff Fletcher's rebuilding effort had yet to bear fruit, and the team was on a three-game losing streak, which started with a 12–1 humiliation in Pittsburgh at the hands of the Penguins.

Hunter needed an early story to fill the space in his newspaper where that night's game story would go in later editions. After the game-day skate, he approached Anderson in the Leaf dressing room.

"Glenn, I'm looking for answers to why the team is doing so badly," Hunter said. "Do you have any answers?"

"I've got lots of answers," Anderson said, which prompted Hunter to sit down beside him and pull out his notebook.

Anderson stared at Hunter and said, "But I'm not going to tell any of them to you."

Three days later, Fletcher made the famous trade for Doug Gilmour, which sparked an eventual rise in the Leafs' fortunes. But Hunter never did go back and ask Anderson if that had been one of his answers.

Ken Dryden succeeded Fletcher as president and GM of the Leafs in 1997. He was short on concrete knowledge about hockey prospects and how to build a team but big on grand ideas. He was also something of a micromanager and loved to plan the ceremonies and presentations before and during games. This included the scripts for long-suffering public address announcer Andy Frost, which were full of portentous language and were often the cause of unintentional hilarity.

Shortly after the Maple Leafs moved into the Air Canada Centre, some of their longest-serving staffers were honoured in short tributes on the jumbo video screen on the new scoreboard. One of the first was an elderly usher, one of the men who started at Maple Leaf Gardens many years ago.

Dryden's tribute was typically florid, gushing on about the man and his loyal service. In fact, it was the sort of flowery language typically associated with obituaries. Given that the advanced age of many of the ushers brought over from the Gardens was the stuff of local legend, it soon became clear most of the people in the crowd assumed the tribute marked the usher's death.

That's when Bob Stellick, the former PR director who came back to help with the move, was seen rushing into the scoreboard operator's booth. He ordered the cameraman to get a shot of the usher, who was sitting proudly near the boards, on the scoreboard immediately.

When asked why, Stellick barked, "Because everybody thinks he's dead!"

On another occasion, a group of women paid a visit to the Air Canada Centre and were accorded official recognition because they were carrying the torch for the 2002 Commonwealth Games in Manchester, England. They were part of the torch relay which would finish in Manchester when the official flame was lit during the opening ceremonies.

The women carried the torch to their seats and held it up for the scoreboard video camera as Andy Frost boomed a salute penned by Dryden over the speakers. Unfortunately, the torch bore an uncanny resemblance to a certain part of the male anatomy, and even more unfortunately, Dryden's script had Frost making reference to the women handling or gripping "the pulsating torch" several times.

This reduced many in the press box, including me, to helpless laughter. At the end of the first period I ran up the stairs to give Frost the usual ribbing after he was forced to read one of Dryden's overblown scripts. Frost was just coming out of his booth and looked grim. He stopped, pointed a finger at me and said, "Don't you start," turned on his heel, and walked out of the press box.

The late Carl Brewer was famous for his battles with management, starting with Punch Imlach on the Leaf teams in the early 1960s through Alan Eagleson, the infamous head of the NHL Players' Association, over the players' pensions in the 1990s. But Brewer had a lighter side, as he was also known for imaginative practical jokes. His best one came when he played for the Toronto Toros in the World Hockey Association in the 1973-74 season.

The Toros had a flight on a Boeing 767, the first time the team, or probably any of the players, had flown on the famous jumbo jet. Brewer got himself bumped to first class for the flight and disappeared into the washroom shortly after takeoff. In the washroom, he stripped down to a bathing suit he had on under his clothes and used a small paper cup to douse himself with water.

After he was soaking wet, Brewer grabbed a towel he brought along, left his clothes and walked back to economy class. As soon as his teammates saw him, Brewer began towelling off.

"Geez, guys," he said, "you should see the great swimming pool we have up in first class."

Errol Thompson, who played on one of the greatest lines in Leaf history with Darryl Sittler and Lanny McDonald in the 1970s, didn't see anything funny in this story at the time. But he doesn't mind telling it now.

The tale starts in February 1978, when the Leafs played a game in Detroit shortly before Thompson and three draft picks were traded to the Red Wings for Dan Maloney, Craig Muni, and a draft pick.

"About a month before I got traded, we were in Detroit," Thompson said. "I was usually the first guy on the bus, and I was sitting there by myself. I saw a policeman run by, and all of a sudden I saw bullets ricocheting off a car roof.

"The policeman was shooting at this guy who was trying to steal a car from the parking lot. I asked myself, 'Why would anyone want to play here?' When I got the phone call about the trade, that was in the back of my mind.

"There were some rumours that I was going to be traded, and my wife at the time said, 'I don't care where we go as long as it's not Detroit.' So when I got the phone call from [GM] Jim Gregory, I never said a word. I hung up the phone, and she said, 'We're going to Detroit, aren't we?'"

There is no shortage of people in the hockey business who have some scars from the marital wars. The travel and hours associated with the game have broken up many a marriage.

But for a guy like Jim Ralph, such discord is a source of humour. Ralph was a goaltender who never cracked the NHL but cracked up his teammates on many junior and minor-league hockey teams. His career also serves as fodder for his humour, but Ralphie notes that few of his coaches found him funny.

Ralph is the analyst on the Leafs radio broadcasts, and one of his funniest lines came during a Leaf broadcast in October 2003. The Leafs were in Montreal, and before the game, the Canadiens held a ceremony to honour Jean Beliveau's 50 years with the organization.

Play-by-play man Joe Bowen was describing the pregame ceremony and then noted that a second banner was being raised, one that marked Beliveau's 50th wedding anniversary, which coincided with the hockey celebration.

Ralph did not miss a beat. "That's one banner they'll never raise for us, Joe," he said.

Al Iafrate was one of the most free-spirited players to ever play for the Maple Leafs. The big defenceman had lots of talent, but focusing on the task at hand was sometimes difficult for him. One of our informants said this cost Iafrate a smack on the head from coach John Brophy during one game.

"Alfie was checking out a chick in the stands once and Brophy caught him," our spy said. "Brophy came up behind him and drilled him, just like that. He said, 'Keep your eyes on the ice, you fucking moron.'"

There was another player on Brophy's teams who vexed him far worse than Iafrate. This fellow had an abundance of talent but little interest in working hard, a combination sure to anger Brophy, who believed in hard work above all.

Also, the player was married but liked to spend time with the groupies who were found in every NHL city. There were two in particular in the New York area this fellow liked, which resulted in a memorable confrontation between the groupies and Brophy. The incident happened after a trying game at Nassau Coliseum against the New York Islanders, where the team hotel was just across the parking lot from the arena.

Our informant says Brophy started a slow burn before the game when the player in question could not be located to fill in for a sick teammate.

"The warm-up is going on and somebody couldn't play," the source said. "But we couldn't find [the player]. Then we paged him on the PA system. I saw him coming in from Marriott and said, 'Where have you been?'

"The guy goes in the dressing room, gets dressed—and he hadn't stretched or anything. So he goes out and on his first or second shift he pulls a muscle because he hadn't stretched. Now he can't play the rest of the game, and Broph is really pissed off.

"After the game, it's pouring rain and Broph is making that 200-yard walk back to the Marriott. Rain was pouring down on his head, and these two bimbos descend on him. They get on him about not playing their boy because they didn't know he got hurt on his first shift.

"Brophy had finally had enough and exploded. He was dropping f-bombs, c-bombs, all that stuff. It was surreal."

Ken Yaremchuk was a Maple Leaf for a brief period until one night early in the 1988-89 season when he made his first trip to Los Angeles with the team. Lotusland was the scene of several Leafs misadventures, and Yaremchuk's started when he had too much to drink.

"L.A. was a big party spot for the guys," a Leafs source said. "They went out one night, and Ken Yaremchuk ended up getting arrested. He was making like a matador with the cars on the street with his jacket. He wouldn't stop, so the cops finally arrested him.

"The kicker was that after he was arrested he said to the cops, 'Don't you know who I am?' After we got him bailed out, we sent him home.

"We played in Calgary the next day, and the entrance to the rink in Calgary was underground, and there was a door with bars. John Kordic ran ahead of everybody and stood there behind the door, shaking the bars and yelling, 'Don't you know who I am? I'm Ken Yaremchuk!' Everybody laughed like hell."

Another of my sources tells the tale of a Leafs coach with an outsized libido. Thanks to his position, he had lots of opportunities to satisfy it.

"A bunch of us were walking down the street in New York one time, talking about strange stuff," he said. "Someone asked, 'How many women have you slept with?' Somebody says, 'This many,' I say, 'That many,' and [the coach] says, 'One thousand.'

"One thousand? And he wasn't bullshitting. Nobody called bullshit on him."

Tie Domi had a hand in many practical jokes during his days with the Maple Leafs. His best one, though, came about because of a stunt Domi had no part in.

One of Domi's teammates had way too much to drink at a team party and passed out. Several other of his teammates thought it would be nice to take off his shirt and write all over his body with a permanent marker. The fellow woke up in the morning with a terrible hangover, looked in the mirror, and saw he was covered in all sorts of witty one-liners.

The player swore revenge and declared Domi the principal target because he was sure Domi was the ringleader. Domi was innocent actually, but word got to him about the player's intentions, so Domi made sure to beat the other player to the Leafs dressing room for practice that day and take preventative measures.

A few minutes later, the prank victim came in, went to Domi's stall, and grabbed all of the hockey gear hanging there. He threw it all in the whirlpool and said to Domi, "That's for writing on me last night, and good luck skating with wet equipment."

The player was confused by Domi's laughter until he double-checked, discovered the switch, and had to fish his own equipment out of the whirlpool.

One Leaf player used a year-end party to write another chapter in his home life, according to someone who was there.

"We had a decent year, and we were having our annual get-together," the source said. "One guy called his wife and said, 'Honey, I won't be home.' She said she understood because it was the year-end bash, you'll be out late, and so on.

"Only this guy said, 'No, you don't understand me. I am not coming home, ever. We are done.'

"That was one hell of a party."

2

THE GLORY YEARS

When Bob Haggert was a young man in his 20s, he was hired as a trainer for the 1954-55 season by Conn Smythe, the founder of the Leafs, and his soon-to-be general manager, Clarence (Hap) Day. Haggert stayed with the team for 14 years, coming aboard when it was floundering in the last years of the Smythe-Day partnership and then working through the glory years of the 1960s under Punch Imlach.

At the end of the 1967-68 season, Haggert went into the business end of sports and left the team. He became president of Sports Representatives Ltd., which handled marketing, licencing, and publishing deals in the sports industry. He is now retired and looks back fondly on his days with the Leafs. "I loved every friggin' moment of it," he says.

Haggert says he even loved working for Smythe, who ran his team with an iron first and nary a sign of a velvet glove. Smythe was a military man who built a sand-and-gravel business too. He headed a group that bought the Toronto St. Pats, a financially wobbly National Hockey League team, on February 14, 1927. Smythe renamed the team the Toronto Maple Leafs and changed their colours to blue and white, the same as those of his beloved University of Toronto. He went on to build Maple Leaf Gardens, the most glittering palace in hockey when it opened in 1931.

Smythe was an unforgiving taskmaster who did not hesitate to fire anyone who was slow to obey an order. He served as the general

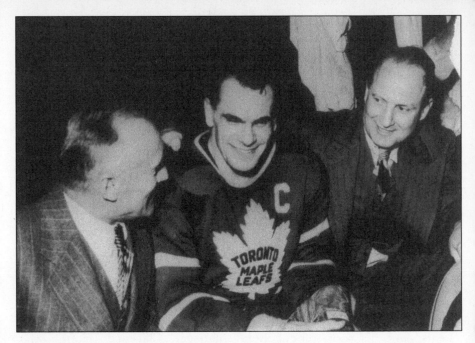

Conn Smythe (left), shown with Leaf captain Syl Apps (centre), was an unforgiving taskmaster along with Hap Day (right).

manager of the Leafs from the day he bought the team until 1955, when he gave the title to Hap Day. Smythe stayed on as president until 1957. Then he ceded control of the franchise to his son, Stafford, Harold Ballard, and John Bassett.

Day spent 31 years with the Maple Leafs as a player, head coach, assistant GM, and GM. Like Smythe, he was an unforgiving martinet, and the two of them were inseparable before a bitter falling out in 1957. Day also worked with Smythe in his sand-and-gravel business (called C. Smythe For Sand) and eventually became a part owner of the company.

No one connected with the Leafs made big money in 1950s, from the training staff to the players. Many of them, including Haggert, worked at Smythe's gravel pit north of Toronto during the summer. Not long after the hockey season ended, Haggert says, you were expected for duty at C. Smythe For Sand.

"In those days, once the season was over, you got two weeks' salary and then [had to] get out," Haggert said. "You had two weeks to make sure everything went out for repair, got this and that done, got the order out to have the dressing room painted. You ordered all your equipment so it was there August 15, and then you went out and found a job.

"Every player worked in the off-season. There were no hockey camps, no hockey schools. That was 20 years later. A few guys worked for the breweries. They'd sit around all day saying, 'Can I buy you one?' That was a great job.

"But the majority of them worked at Smythe's sand pit. Everybody worked out there as labourers. You had stars of the Toronto Maple Leafs shoveling rock."

As he was with the Leafs, Smythe the gravel pit owner was the absolute commander, and Day was his second-in-command. Both men started early and worked late.

"Hap Day would be on the grounds by six o'clock in the morning," Haggert said. "He would be driving around the pits. You had to take samples of sand, gravel, and rock. They had special machines to dissect the quality. Day would be in every morning doing that.

"Conn Smythe had a garage under his office with a secret staircase from the garage to his office. He could be in there for two or three hours and you wouldn't know he was on the property. Then you would hear his cane hit a desk and it was, 'Good morning, Mr. Smythe. How are you, sir?'

"I lived downtown by Maple Leaf Gardens and, boy, that was a long hike on streetcars to get there by 7 a.m. But if you were five minutes late, you were dead. Their theory was, 'If we can be on time, you can be on time.'

"And they were right."

One summer, Haggert was given the job of running the weigh scale at the gravel pit. Smythe had his own way of doing things at the pit, just like he did with the Leafs, which Haggert discovered early in his time at the scale.

"Conn Smythe's office had a window that looked out on the scale," Haggert said. "And of course he had those stairs from the garage to his office. If the door was shut, you didn't know if he was in, and that was the way he wanted it.

"Unlike the labourers, the truck drivers were all independent. They got paid by the load, so the more you hustled, the more you made. Before you could get authorized for another load, you had to bring your empty truck up on the scale.

"There was a sign by the scale—'All loads must be levelled by the driver so they are flat at the top and not mounded. Trucks cannot be measured by the scale man unless the top is flat.'"

Smythe installed the rule because a truck with a load of sand or stone that was in a mound at the top would lose some of it when the truck turned the corner from the company driveway to the street. When debris fell on the street, officials from the city would threaten to issue Smythe a fine.

"So Conn Smythe says I'll eliminate that," Haggert said. "I won't allow trucks to leave unless the driver gets out, climbs up on top and flattens out the load himself."

This did not endear Smythe to the drivers, who regarded any delay as money spent out of their pockets. But a rule was a rule, as Haggert soon found out.

"There was one really hot day, and the drivers are pushing, saying, 'If I can get ten loads today, I can buy a yacht.' Guys like Bob Pulford and Bobby Baun did this job. I'm now doing this job, and I know what that sign says.

"Guys would drive up, and I'd open the window and get their ticket. I'd read the scale, subtract the weight of their empty truck, and figure how much their load was. But I could never stamp their ticket until they levelled their load. I'd say, 'I can't let you go. You have to get up on that truck and level the sand off. There's a sign.'

"The driver would say, 'Screw the sign, I don't give a damn. Come out here, kid, and I'll kick your ass.' These guys were tough. They were on time, and they didn't want to get up and shovel crushed rock around the truck. They'd say, 'Haggert, you're gonna want a ride home tonight. Well you ain't getting one from me.'

"The other drivers in line would be honking their horns. They're yelling, 'What are you doing Haggert, you little jerk? Why don't you let him go?' It would be a big fight."

Finally, on that hot, hot day, Haggert was worn down enough to relent.

"I said, 'Yeah, go ahead,' to one guy. I did not know Conn Smythe was in his office. The truck went off the scale past Smythe's window. The whole staff was there. The truck didn't get 15 feet and Smythe came out of his office with his cane. The cane hit a desk, and I damn near had a heart attack. Now I knew he was here, and I knew he caught me."

Smythe roared at Haggert.

"Haggert! Stop the line, go out and get that last truck that went by my window. Make him back it up in front of my window, and make him level the load. Now!"

This was not a prospect Haggert relished. The drivers were not averse to getting rough. But he knew there was no other choice.

"So I gathered myself up, because Conn was watching, and yelled, 'Hey, you, back your truck up.' Now I was full of it.

"'Make me,' the driver said. Oh, God, don't say that to me, I'm thinking. So I said, 'Listen, Conn's watching. If you don't want to lose your licence, if you want to do business here, back up.'

"The guy's going, 'Yeah, yeah, you're a jerk.' And does he take his time backing up, because he knows Conn's watching. Then it was up on the truck, shovel a little here, a little there, taking his time. Trucks were honking, drivers were yelling.

"Finally, he got the load levelled. I gave him his ticket, and I went in the office."

That's when he discovered Smythe was not finished yet.

"Conn says, 'Bob Haggert!'

"Yes, sir!"

"'Go outside, get that sign, and bring it in my office.'

"Well, the sign was as big as this table," Haggert said, indicating the large antique dining table in his Toronto home. "I had to go outside and unhook the sign. I brought it in, and he said, 'Put it up on the table. I'll hold it.'

"He was holding it and said, 'Now I want you to read it to me.' I read, 'All loads must be levelled, et cetera, et cetera.' I knew it word for word.

"He said, 'You seem to know what it says.' I said yes, and he said, 'Well, you don't seem to understand something. If that truck goes out on the highway and spills sand on the road, I could lose my licence.'

"He said, 'You know what? The next truck that goes by my window with a mound, you're fired. Now get back to work.' So I had to go back out with the sign and hang it up."

Naturally, it took just a few seconds for word to go around the gravel pit that Haggert took a major tongue-lashing from The Major, as Smythe was known.

"Guys working in the yard were George Armstrong, Tod Sloan, Jimmy Thomson—real hard pros," Haggert said. "When the shift was over at five o'clock, they all decided to march up to the office. They got in the room and they couldn't stop laughing. 'Haggert got caught,' they all said.

"But you learned from things like that. I was in my early 20s, and it was the best experience."

Down at Maple Leaf Gardens, Smythe and Day were just as demanding. They were the absolute bosses. King Clancy was the coach when Haggert was hired in 1954, but he was the court jester of the regime, serving under various titles over the years and filling in as coach when someone got fired. Howie Meeker took over from Clancy in 1956, but he only lasted one season, giving way to Billy Reay, who got in 90 games before Punch Imlach arrived in 1959. Imlach became the next Gardens dictator, but by then Smythe had stepped down as president.

Under Smythe and Day there were rules for everything from how the players dressed to their personal hygiene.

"You shaved at home, not after the practice or the game," Haggert said. "They didn't have all that crap in the dressing room they do now. You came to Maple Leaf Gardens in a shirt and tie, suit, or blazer. Every day. None of this jeans or ball caps on backwards stuff.

"Smythe and Day would be there, always looking around to see what was going on. If you didn't dress properly, you'd get fined. You can't fine anybody today because the NHLPA will file a grievance."

One player who learned the hard way about breaking Smythe's rules was John (Goose) McCormack. He had the temerity to ignore this commandment—thou shalt not get married during the hockey season.

McCormack was a checking centre from Edmonton who played on the 1951 Stanley Cup champion Leafs. During the following season, McCormack got married but neglected both to ask Smythe's permission and to tell him after the fact.

"The players all knew, but Smythe didn't," Haggert said. "Smythe found out and demoted him the next day. Can you imagine that?

"You don't get married during the season. Then everybody got on Conn's ass, saying, 'How bad can you be?' But it didn't bother him. He said, 'Rules are rules, and I make them up.'"

Things did not work out too badly for McCormack, though. He was eventually traded to the Montreal Canadiens, where he played for the next three seasons. He was on the 1952-53 team, which won the Stanley Cup, although McCormack did not get in any of the playoff games.

Smythe and Day's intransigence extended to every employee of the Gardens. They ran the operations at the arena as tightly they did at C. Smythe For Sand.

"Smythe and Day were like Frick and Frack," Haggert said. "They both put in the same hours at the gravel pit and Maple Leaf Gardens. Day would come in the Gardens at six in the morning, and he'd walk the building. He would start at the top. He'd go in every washroom, every concession stand. Those floors were scrubbed every day, and if you couldn't eat off that floor, there was trouble. He'd go through the building by section. He'd start at the greys then go to the greens, the blues, and then the reds.

"When he was done, he would go to his office and phone the electrician. He'd say, 'There's a light bulb out in the women's washroom in the greys, section 43, and I saw another here, here, and here.' Then he'd say, 'It's eight o'clock in the morning. You've got an hour. Get 'em all done.'

"Man, was it clean in those days. Just unbelievable. And Conn and Hap would stand there with big grins; they were so proud of the Gardens."

Smythe believed that fear was the greatest motivator of all. A constant state of worry about your job produced the best results seemed to be his motto.

"Everybody would fear to God when Conn was in the building," Haggert said. "He would come in off Wood Street in his big Cadillac with his cane. There was a buzzer at the Wood Street entrance, and Conn would go in there at two in the morning if he was making deals.

"He'd press the buzzer, and if that door wasn't going up in 10 seconds, and he had to press the buzzer a second time, the guy on duty was automatically fired. Sometimes the night guy was off smoking somewhere or having a couple of drinks. But Smythe could come rolling in at three in the morning. You had to be ready.

"'Good evening, Mr. Smythe, how are you?' the night man would say.

"'Good evening, Mr. Watchman, how's everything?'

"'Just fine sir, couldn't be better.'

"Someone was watching someone every day of the week around there," Haggert said.

Day's obsession for order was particularly acute when it came to the order of everts. He was a stickler for schedules, and to that end, he had a ritual every morning at the Gardens after his building inspection was finished.

"There was a guy who was the building manager, Don (Shanty) McKenzie," Haggert said. "He played football for the Toronto Argonauts. His off-season job was to be the building manager.

"At 10:30 in the morning, Hap Day would go in the dressing room and phone Shanty McKenzie and tell him to come over to the dressing room. Shanty would come over with a clipboard and stopwatches."

That was also the command for McKenzie to telephone the Royal Observatory in England, which kept Greenwich Mean Time. He would get the official time and synchronize it with his stopwatches. Then McKenzie would join Day in the rink, where there were a clock and two flags at each end, hanging behind the goals.

"Hap Day would set each clock at the end of the building by the second. And he would set his watch. You could give birth to his time."

Once all watches and clocks were synchronized, Day would turn to the next order of business, which was a team meeting at 11 a.m. on the morning of a game. The players all had to be through the door of the dressing room on the dot, according to Greenwich Mean Time, or else.

"Day would stand outside the dressing room, watching guys come in," Haggert said. "There would always be a couple of idiots who didn't leave early enough, or it was snowing, or whatever. And the clock would be going tick tick tick.

"These players would be running around the ends of the building trying to get to the dressing room. They'd get this close, but it was 11 o'clock. Hap Day would shut the door and lock it, right on the second.

"So the players would bang on the door, and Day would open it.

"'What do you want?'

"'Oh, I took the streetcar,' 'It was snowing,' or, 'I couldn't get a parking spot.'

"Bam! would go the door. That would get Day really upset, so he'd lay into everybody. When he was finished, he would open the door. The two players would be there and say, 'Hey, Mr. Day [you never called him Hap], what's going on?'

"He would point at the other players and say, 'Ask them. They got here on time.'"

This is when the culprits would get a taste of Hap Day justice. He carried around form letters to serve him in this, and the letters involved the Ontario Society for Crippled Children, which just happened to be the charity for which Smythe was a driving force.

"Day would reach into his pocket," Haggert said, "and say, 'Oh, by the way, gentlemen, here's one for you and one for you.' He would give each one of them a letter. The players would open the letters which would say, 'Dear Whomever, The Ontario Society for Crippled Children would like to thank you for your donation to the children's village. One hundred dollars will be deducted from your salary immediately.'

"While Day was giving his speech to the players, he would be writing your name on the letter."

In today's NHL, teams have a morning skate on the day of the game. The players put on all of their equipment and have a light practice for between 30 and 40 minutes.

When Smythe ran the Maple Leafs, there was a skate, but it was only for a few minutes, and it followed the 11 o'clock meeting. Haggert says this practice was introduced by Smythe and, like everything else about the team, it was for a reason.

"Conn Smythe was the first guy to start the 11 o'clock meetings," Haggert said. "They would only be held at home, not on the road. One reason was so the players would have to get out of bed and not sleep until noon or one o'clock.

"The other purpose was for the players to put on their skates. They wore their suits and ties, they took their sticks, skated two or three times around the ice, and came off. This was only for one reason: Tommy Naylor was the guy who sharpened your skates, so if you had a complaint, they wanted to hear about it then, not at game time."

The players would just skate around and say, "Yeah, I'm good."

There is no definitive story about how today's custom of the morning skate began. Most NHL people agree the practice started in the 1960s, but there are varying stories about its origin. Haggert believes the morning skate began in the early 1960s when Chicago Blackhawks coach Rudy Pilous wanted to rein in his players, who had a passion for fun.

"Our teams never practiced on game day, and Toe Blake's teams [the Montreal Canadiens] didn't either," Haggert said. "The guy who started that was Rudy Pilous. Rudy was a throwback from the old days.

"The Blackhawks were in Montreal at the Mount Royal Hotel. That Chicago team liked to have a good time. On the night before the game, Rudy smelled something was up. So either he or someone he hired sat in the lobby, and at 5:30 in the morning, in come the big boys.

"Rudy got up around nine o'clock and phoned every room. He said there was a practice at 11 o'clock. The Blackhawks had never practiced before on the day of the game. Guys were stinking of booze, and he drove the crap out of them.

"Montreal beat them 7–1, so Rudy vowed never again on the road would his team get that kind of freedom."

The road trips were run on a strict schedule, and the man in charge of that schedule was Day. His preoccupation with punctuality meant the itinerary was rigid, and this extended to the train conductors, who thought they knew a thing or two about the correct time themselves.

It was not uncommon for the Maple Leafs to play at home and then leave by train a couple hours later for an overnight ride to a road game.

"When the players came in for the 11 o'clock meeting, Hap Day would hand them the itinerary," Haggert said. "It would say, 'The game is at 8:30 tonight, and the train leaves sharply at 12 o'clock from Union Station.'

"The itinerary would say, 'Here's where we're staying in Chicago,' for example, 'here's the train times and the phone numbers.' The itinerary was handed out so the guys could give it to their wives.

"The game was usually over around 10:30 and the train would leave at midnight. The players had to find their own way to the train station. There were no team buses. So guys' wives, girlfriends, pals, whoever, would take them to the station. Somehow you got there.

"Players had to carry two pairs of skates and their overnight bag. Wives and girlfriends would put sandwiches and three or four beers in your overnight bag, because often you couldn't get food anywhere."

When Day arrived at the station, he would go through a similar ritual with his watch as he did with Shanty McKenzie and the Gardens clocks. But this time, Haggert served as his assistant.

"I had to look after a whole pile of stuff, so by the time I got to the station it was always quarter to 12," Haggert said. "Hap Day would go, 'Bobby, get the conductor.' There was always a conductor and a brakeman, and they'd put the caboose on the back of the last car of the train, a private car reserved for Leafs players.

"I'd fetch the conductor, and Day would say, 'What time is your watch, Mr. Train Man? The guy would pull out his watch, Hap Day would pull out his watch and say, 'You're two minutes fast.' Oh, that would piss the train guy off."

What followed was sometimes a reprise of the 11 o'clock meetings from Day's tenure as coach.

"Now guys would be running down the platform at one minute to 12," Haggert said. "You'd see guys coming, they'd be 300 feet down the platform and the train was leaving. Day would say, 'Conductor, what time have you got?' By then, the conductor had matched his watch to Day's.

"He would tell the conductor to close up and start the train. The conductor would give one last all-aboard. Now you would see guys running faster than Ben Johnson. Some would make it, some wouldn't."

There were no repeat offenders among those who missed the train. The consequences ensured that.

"You only missed it once," Haggert said. "If you missed it, you had to find your own way to get where we were going. And there were no airplanes. It was a nice all-night and all-day drive to Chicago."

Once the guilty party arrived at the team hotel, he would be handed a note that ordered him to call Day in his room.

"You would be told to come on up," Haggert said. "Day would say, 'We've got a problem here: I can make it, everybody on the train can make it, but not you.' And then he'd get warmed up.

"After he was finished, he would say, 'Well, anyway, I'm glad you made it. Tonight, you can go back home on the train with us.' Then he'd say, 'I don't know how much it cost you to get here. I don't care. But here's a letter.' And that one would say, 'The Ontario Society of Crippled Children would like to thank you for your kind donation of 500 dollars.'"

"Some guys there, the rookies, were making eighteen hundred, twenty-three hundred a year, something like that. But that wouldn't bother Hap at all. It was all business.

Talk of train travel today by sports teams always evokes a sense of nostalgia for a more leisurely era, when the players formed tight bonds over hours of conversation and card games in a Pullman car, rather than cat-napping on one-hour airplane flights.

As one whose job it was to ensure the team's equipment as well as the players got on the train on time, however, Haggert will tell you it didn't seem romantic at the time. In fact, there was one practice left over from World War II that made train trips a pain in the neck.

"During the war years there was great worry about travelling by train," Haggert said. "There was a fear the Germans could get on a train, if it was travelling across the border, and cause all sorts of havoc."

This meant much greater scrutiny of cross-border trains by United States and Canadian customs and immigration officials, something people living in a post-9/11 world can understand. This scrutiny persisted into the 1950s and led to an unusual routine for Haggert and his fellow trainer, Tommy Naylor.

"To cope with the customs inspections, the Toronto Maple Leafs and the Montreal Canadiens had two sets of hockey equipment," Haggert said. "We were the only two teams in the National Hockey League that did because we crossed the border the most.

"If we were playing at home on Saturday night and on Sunday night in Chicago, we'd take the overnight train. But you would send a set of equipment to Chicago on Wednesday. You would send everything except the skates. I had to go to the train station on Wednesday because the customs and immigration officers would go through everything and seal it. Then the trainer in Chicago would send a truck down to the train and get the equipment. He would call and say, 'Your equipment is here, it's stored, and don't worry about it.'

"When the game was over, every player had to carry two pairs of skates to the train. We were also the only teams where players had a spare pair of skates. You had the pair you wore that night, and under the bench was your spare pair."

Smythe's rules did not end with his employees. Even his paying customers were subject to them. A night at Maple Leaf Gardens, in Smythe's view, was as important as a night at the theatre or the opera.

People were expected to, and did, dress accordingly, particularly in the red seats, the most expensive ones. At the minimum, gentlemen were expected to wear suits. The ladies wore evening gowns and furs. If the season-ticket holders did not meet the dress code, or if they gave their tickets away to someone who did not—legend says the family maid and her boyfriend were the usual culprits—they would hear about it.

"Five minutes after the game started, the box office manager and one or two of his assistants had to walk around the reds," Haggert said. "He had a pad and pencil and would mark it down—box 42, row 6, seat whatever, no shirt and tie.

"This stopped sometime in the '60s, but in Smythe's day it was done for every game. If you were a man and wife and you went to the game, it wasn't a game, it was an occasion. It was Saturday night, and the women wore fur coats. The men wore black coats or cashmere coats and a shirt and tie. All of the men wore fedoras.

"The box office manager, who was a guy named Gord Finn, would go around and write up people who had no shirt and tie. He knew the seatholders because he did it twice a week. Then he would go look up the seatholder in the records and say, 'Yep, it wasn't him. He must have given the tickets away.'

"So he'd phone the guy on Monday morning. 'Hello, Mr. Smith, how are you? Did you enjoy the game?'

"'Oh yes.'

"And this is where he'd get them. 'Well, sir,' he'd say, 'I checked your box at the game, and I didn't see you.' There'd be dead silence.

"Then Gord Finn would say, 'You weren't in your box. Someone was there who didn't have a shirt and tie on. If it happens again, we'll take your tickets back.'

"Conn Smythe made sure the Toronto Maple Leafs were the class of the league. He figured, 'If you are going to come to my building and watch my team, you're going to dress properly.' He set the standard very high.

"But you know what? Guys loved getting dressed up and taking their wives out. Their wives may not have loved going to hockey games, but oh dear, they loved getting a new fur coat, or going out dancing afterward.

"It was a different time, but they made sure everybody was on the ball. Smythe and Day made sure everybody was accountable."

The dress code at Maple Leaf Gardens was enforced down to the maintenance workers who operated the resurfacing machines on the ice. In the days before the ubiquitous Zamboni, the ice was cleaned and resurfaced between periods by men pulling large barrels of water that sat on sleds.

"The guys who cleaned the ice all had to wear the same thing," Haggert said. "Black slacks, white cardigan, and blue tie. Nowadays, could you ever catch some guy in Nashville or Atlanta doing that? But guys fought for that job."

Naturally, in keeping with Smythe's military background, the barrels had to be pulled in the same formation.

"They'd go down the middle together for the last circle and the out the door in the north end," Haggert said. "We had the best ice in the league. Us and Montreal."

In the days before the National Hockey League Players' Association, Conn Smythe and his fellow NHL owners treated the players as chattel. They were sent to the minor leagues or traded as punishment for various transgressions as often as they were for strategic reasons. If you did not toe the line, you were gone.

An early attempt to form a players union was crushed when Smythe and the other owners traded the players who were behind the movement. Jimmy Thomson, a loyal Leaf for more than ten years, and Tod Sloan, also a ten-year man and one of the best players on the team, were traded to the Chicago Blackhawks, hockey's Siberia.

Haggert recalls another capricious exercise in power during the mid-1950s, when the team was struggling. Hap Day decided to provide his team with some incentive to break a losing streak.

"We didn't have a very good team," Haggert said. "We had lost five straight and were coming home from somewhere. It was Saturday before a home game, and Hap was beyond angry. We knew not to go near him.

"At the morning meeting, he went into the dressing room and he gave it to them. He called the players everything in the book. He said, 'Look around the dressing room, boys.' Back then, we carried 18 players, and Day said, 'We've got 20 players here. We've got two too many. I want you to know something. If we lose tonight, two players are going to Pittsburgh after the game.'"

In the 1950s, the Pittsburgh Hornets were the Leafs' primary farm team. It was a long drop in prestige from the Maple Leafs to the

Hornets, both in pay and playing conditions.

Haggert says Day ended his speech with an added incentive: the tickets to Pittsburgh are by train and they are one-way.

"You're going and you ain't coming back," Day said.

"We lose, Day comes in, and whomp goes the door," Haggert said. "Everybody's jittery. Day said, 'I guess you guys didn't listen to what I said this morning. Larry Cahan and Bob Solinger, take your skates and sticks, here's your one-way tickets to Pittsburgh. Have a good season.'

"They went over, picked up their skates, and Day said, 'By the way, you're only allowed to take three sticks with you.' He never shook hands with them, nothing. He just said, 'See you at training camp.'

"And this was the middle of the season. The room went dead silent. Problem solved."

Aside from hockey and gravel, Conn Smythe's other great passion was horse racing. His silks were blue and white, of course, and his stable grew along with his profits from the Maple Leafs and C. Smythe For Sand. According to Leafs legend, however, it was one of Smythe's first horses that allowed him to launch his reign over the Toronto hockey scene and the NHL.

After Smythe bought the Leafs, he had big plans but little cash to realize them. By 1930, he wanted to build a grand palace for his team, and he wanted a star attraction on the team to draw enough paying customers to help pay the bills.

There was such a player available, defenceman Frank (King) Clancy of the Ottawa Senators. The Senators were in even worse financial shape than the Leafs, and they were willing to sell Clancy to Smythe for $35,000. That was a lot of money in those days, money that Smythe didn't quite have.

What Smythe did have was a horse, a filly named Rare Jewel that was said to have cost him only $250. Rare Jewel's racing record was as modest as her price, but a jockey, Dude Foden, told Smythe the horse was far better than her record. Smythe was convinced and entered the horse in one of the biggest races of the day, the Coronation Futurity. Then he put down as many bets as he could on his horse.

Rare Jewel came through at long odds, and Smythe won a total of $14,000. That gave Smythe enough cash to meet the purchase price on Clancy, who stayed with the organization for more than 50 years. Within a year, Smythe had Maple Leaf Gardens under construction.

Despite the unforgiving nature of Smythe, he inspired great loyalty in his employees. One reason, Haggert says, was his practice of opening his country estate in what is now Caledon, Ontario, for a riotous party once a year for all the Gardens employees, from the players on down.

After Smythe extracted all of the sand and rock he could from his pit in the north end of Toronto, he turned his hand to real-estate development and house construction. The sand pit was turned into a large subdivision, and Smythe formed a new company, C. Smythe For Homes, that built all the houses.

Smythe then moved his sand and gravel operation to the hills of Caledon, where there was a large supply of raw material. He also built himself an imposing mansion.

"For years they had a deal where every summer, every employee at Maple Leaf Gardens, from the guy who cleaned the washrooms to the president, went up to Smythe's house in Caledon," Haggert said. "You could have everything you could eat and drink. And for one day you could call your boss anything you want. But that was it, one day.

"Well, the guys who were the cleaners, they were drinking triple scotches with both hands and two in their pockets. They couldn't get enough. Guys were in the swimming pool, guys' shorts were falling off. This was the day you got even.

"Smythe had some hotel chefs come out with a buffet, and they were slicing the beef. There was a famous piano player, an entertainer, he'd come out and sing Smythe's favourite song, something that went, 'Come around any old time, make yourself at home, ta da, ta da.' Guys would be crying."

Haggert says the 1958 party was particularly memorable because it was shortly after one of Smythe's horses, Caledon Beau, won the Queen's Plate, the biggest horse race in Canada. Horse racing may be on the decline now, but in the 1950s it was not uncommon for members of the Royal Family to show up and present the winning prize.

"When the party was in full swing," Haggert said, "Smythe came in the room and said, 'Ladies and gentlemen, bring your drinks outside.' We went outside, and down this tree-lined laneway came a big tractor-trailer with the Queen's Plate winner on it. The truck circled around in front of Smythe, the door was dropped, and out comes the horse.

"He said, 'When we won the Queen's Plate, the Queen gave me this big bottle of champagne,' and it was big, and Smythe said, 'I never opened it. I saved it for this day to share with you.'

"Well, there wasn't a dry eye within 50 miles. Then he popped it. Guys were crying and drinking, because he was sharing. We were family.

"'We won. We're going to drink the champagne together. We're Toronto Maple Leafs together.'

"When the guys went back to work, Smythe could have said I want you to work 500 straight hours, and they would have said, 'When do we start?' He did that every summer, every July. A lot went into the building of that franchise. Now they talk about marketing synergy and cross-promotion.

"How about frigging winning?"

While there were lots of times he may have smarted under the whip of Smythe and Day, from the vantage point of 50 years later, Haggert says they were great days.

"I was from a single-parent home, and I learned all about life," he said. "Boy, was Day ever tough. The guys who got caught in something hated him, of course, but the guys who didn't thought he was a pretty good guy.

"What Smythe and Day taught was discipline. Everything was calculated, nothing was left for chance. 'You are a Toronto Maple Leaf player, this is how you dress during the day.' 'We're on time, you're on time.'

"But everybody was treated well. We stayed at the best hotels, ate the best food, had a private train car. I loved every minute of it. I worked for Conn Smythe, Hap Day, and Punch Imlach for 14 years. It taught me a lot of values."

One other thing about Smythe was he had an odd definition of loyalty, just like almost every other NHL owner of the time. It only ran one way, from the player to Smythe and the team. Everyone found that out sooner or later, even Hap Day.

Day was Smythe's most loyal associate. He was one of the players when Smythe bought the team, rising to coach in 1940. When Smythe was away leading the Sportsmen's Battery in World War II, Day remained loyal to Smythe when a couple of his fellow directors at the Gardens tried to force him out.

Smythe, who came back from France with some shrapnel in his back that would plague him for the rest of his life, outfoxed his enemies in the spring of 1945. He convinced a couple of directors who were friendly with him to sell their shares to him. That gave Smythe the majority of the Gardens shares, which allowed him to become president in 1947 and cemented his authority.

After that, people thought Day and Smythe would be together forever. Forever lasted until 1957 when Day was 57 years old. By then, Stafford Smythe, Conn's son, was pushing for a greater role in the Maple Leafs and he was not a big fan of Day's way of doing things. The fact the Leafs had not won a Cup since 1951 and finished out of the playoffs in 1956-57 was more ammunition for him.

While Conn Smythe's intentions in what followed remain murky, it is clear that both men's rigidity led to their split in March 1957. The end came when Smythe insulted Day during a press conference with the Toronto hockey writers.

Author Jack Batten, in his book The Leafs, described how the men's relationship blew up:

"I haven't lost confidence in Hap Day," Smythe [told the Toronto reporters]. "He's my general manager, and he'll be asked if he's available to carry on."

In Toronto, Day picked up on the poisoned adjective in Smythe's statement.

"It's odd that I should be asked if I was 'available' after 30 years," Day said. "But since I was asked, I don't want the job anymore."

Haggert says Day's resignation dominated the news that spring.

"It was the big story," he said. "There were five or six pages about it in the papers every day. Later, Conn tried to say he really didn't mean it. He tried to do a little backpedaling but Day said no, he was done.

"Those guys guy were together 30 years. Day, as a player, coach, and manager, had seven Stanley Cups.

"Hap Day could look like he was nothing but mean-spirited. After you got to know him, though, he was a fabulous guy."

After he left the Leafs, Day bought a company in St. Thomas, Ontario, that made axe handles. He ran it for the next 20 years and then turned it over to his son. In 1990, Day passed away in his sleep at the age of 88.

Conn Smythe did not stay at the helm of the Maple Leafs for long after the falling out with Day. He kept the title of president for a few more years but within a few months of Day's departure both the hockey and business decisions were taken over by Stafford Smythe and Harold Ballard. Conn Smythe officially parted with the Gardens in 1961 when he sold controlling interest in the company to his son, Ballard, and John Bassett.

Conn Smythe spent most of his time running his horse-racing operation and it was a long time before Haggert saw him again.

"I guess it was maybe five years after he sold out that he was at a game," Haggert said. "He walked up to me and said, 'Bobby, how are you?'

"I said, 'Fine, Mr. Smythe.'

"He said. 'You can call me Conn.' I was stunned. He said, 'I've always wanted to tell you that.'"

Conn Smythe died on November 18, 1980, at the age of 85.

The turnaround in the Leafs' fortunes began in 1958 when Stafford Smythe and Ballard hired George (Punch) Imlach. Like Hap Day, Imlach was a combative man, even though his nickname was bestowed on him by a sports writer who thought he looked punch drunk after taking a big hit in a hockey game.

Imlach, a Toronto native, was the general manager and coach of the Springfield Indians in the American Hockey League when the Leafs hired him as assistant general manager. Before that, he was the GM and coach of the Quebec Aces, a successful senior hockey team, for ten years.

By the end of his first season, 1958-59, Imlach took over the vacant GM's post and then fired coach Billy Reay, taking over that job as well. In the next ten years, until Stafford Smythe fired him after an embarrassing playoff loss to the Boston Bruins, Imlach and the Leafs won four Stanley Cups.

Haggert says Imlach was another taskmaster, just like Hap Day, but also "a good guy to work for. I worked for him for ten years, and he treated me right."

As the 1960s proceeded into the era of protest and questioning authority, many of the players did not come to share Haggert's view. But Imlach was the absolute boss to the end.

"As long as you knew he was the boss, you had no troubles," Haggert said. "Guys today say, 'I wouldn't put up with that,' and I say, 'Oh yeah?'

"That's the way it was. It's nice 50 years later to say I wouldn't put up with that, but it was the same as under Smythe and Day. Guys would go to the minors and you wouldn't come back until someone died. It was a different time, a different game, different rules. Everybody knew his role."

Imlach turned out to be a brilliant manager and coach. He turned the Leafs around almost immediately.

"We didn't know him personally when he came, but we knew quite a bit about him," Haggert said. "He was a player, then a coach of the Quebec Aces, and then the GM. So when he came to us, for 25 years he had been running every aspect of a team.

"He was a brilliant GM, and he and Toe Blake [of the Montreal Canadiens] were the two best coaches in the league, bar none. I liked working for him because you knew all the time where you stood. There was nothing wishy-washy about him. If you disobeyed him, which I did a couple of times, he didn't speak to you for a couple of weeks.

"The weird part about that was a small part of the trainer's room was where Imlach changed for practice. We were in the same room all the time, and he'd go for ten days and wouldn't say hello. Then we'd be on the road some time and he'd say, 'Let's go for dinner,' and we were back to normal."

Today's NHL coaches wear warm-up suits on the ice for practice, along with hockey gloves and a stick. Imlach, who would arrive at his office early in the morning to carry out the general manager's portion of his portfolio, was much more formal.

"He'd come right from his office, to the trainer's room," Haggert said. "He had a cubicle in our room. He would take off his suit coat and put a jacket on, put his ball cap on and leather gloves, not hockey gloves. Then away he went.

"He kept his shirt and tie on underneath. He didn't wear track suits, sweat suits, windbreakers, or scarves, or any of that crap. Then he would skate around and yell and scream at guys.

"I liked him because he was tough, and to win you've gotta have a leader. There was no question he was the leader."

Imlach was also highly superstitious. This manifested itself in all sorts of ways, from what he wore to his daily schedule. During the Leafs' Stanley Cup run in 1967, an unexpected championship that also turned out to be their last for more than 40 years, Imlach wore an ugly green sports jacket to every game because the Leafs won the first time he wore it.

"People sent him shamrocks and things like that," Haggert said. "He had this in this pocket, that in that pocket. He'd touch certain hockey sticks."

Imlach believed the numbers 7 and 11 brought good luck. Before every game he would go to the bin in the dressing room and tap the sticks belonging to No. 7 for the Leafs, star defenceman Tim Horton, and No. 11, a number that was used by a variety of players over the years.

"It didn't matter who the players were," Haggert said of this custom. "Imlach and I were always the last to leave the dressing room, and he'd tap the sticks on his way out.

"I had to be the last out because I had to lock the door. Imlach would say, 'Come on,' then go over to the bin where all the sticks were and tap 7 and 11. He also had lucky pennies and other coins."

This was mildly amusing to Haggert until the day one of the reporters covering the team wrote about Imlach's superstitions in his newspaper.

"Well, you should have seen the bags of stuff that came in the dressing room," Haggert said. "People sent them in and said, here's my lucky jockstrap, here's my lucky bra. You couldn't stop the flood, and he never threw anything out.

"It's all still in bags somewhere. I don't know where it went. I threw the stuff out of the dressing room finally. It was funny for a while, but then it got to be a pain in the ass."

Under Imlach, the Leafs followed a strict routine on the road, just as they did in the Conn Smythe years.

"It was a ritual," Haggert said. "The game was at eight o'clock, the game-day meal was at one o'clock and you'd better show up on time. Everybody ate the same thing—steak, baked potato, peas, corn, toast, chocolate ice cream, and milk. We didn't have coffee; that wasn't allowed, and neither was tea.

"Imlach would come down and have dinner. So would the trainers. Everybody ate together because we were a team. Then the players would have a three-, four-hour nap. The bus would leave at 6:30. You got to the rink so your players were there maybe 45 minutes before a game. Imlach didn't want you there two, three hours before [getting nervous]. Guys would get there, get dressed, and go on the ice. Now, guys get there at four or five o'clock. God knows what they do with all that time."

On a couple of occasions, Imlach's superstitions played a role in his routines. Haggert and his fellow trainer, Tommy Naylor, got caught up in Imlach's obsession along with Imlach's sidekick, King Clancy.

"After the meal, Tommy Naylor and I would go up to Punch's suite and figure out what the hell we were going to do for the afternoon," Haggert said. "If it was early in the season, we'd watch the NFL, maybe the odd movie on Sunday afternoons. One time in Chicago, Imlach wanted to go to the movies.

"I said, 'Okay, we'll see you later,' and Imlach said, 'No, no, you and Tommy are coming with me and King.'

"We went down the street to the old Chicago Theatre on State Street. I cannot tell you what was playing. Imlach bought the tickets, and I was thinking, 'Oh boy, a free movie.' When we went in, Imlach stopped and said to Clancy, 'Eleven, seven.'

"So Clancy counted down 11 rows and over seven seats. Imlach sat in the seventh seat. Not the sixth or eighth—the seventh. And the rest of you, good luck to you, sit where you want. That night, we beat Chicago."

Imlach made a connection between the two events.

"Three weeks later, we went back to Chicago and we were on a pretty good winning streak. I think we were first or second in the league at the time.

"After dinner at one o'clock, Tommy and I were planning to do something or other. But Imlach came along and said, 'Hey, we're going to the movies. Tommy, King, let's go.' We got our coats, and I'm not thinking at all. We went along State Street to the Chicago Theatre. King got the tickets and the same movie was playing.

"Imlach said, 'King, eleven, seven.' Clancy goes through the same routine, but there's a guy sitting in the seventh seat. I looked at Tommy Naylor and I really wanted to pee my pants laughing. But if I did, Punch would fire me.

"Imlach said, 'King, tell the guy to get out of the seat.' King no more wants to do that than I do, but he had no choice. The boss had spoken. And there were other people sitting in the row. King worked his way down the row and asked the guy if he'd move over. He gave him a line like, 'There's four of us. I'm with my boss, and we'd like to sit together.' The guy said no.

"By now the show was on, Punch was standing up and people were yelling to sit down. I was edging closer to the exit. I didn't want to end up in something. Imlach was steaming. 'I want that seat,' he said. So back went King.

"Now, the other guy was getting belligerent: 'Who do you think you are, coming in off the street, telling me to move?' This argument went on for ten minutes, and the guy wouldn't give up his seat. The rest of the people weren't too happy either. Finally, Imlach threw his hands up and said, 'Let's go, come on, King.' We went outside and there was another theatre down the street.

"Imlach said, 'Let's go to the show down here.' We went in, Imlach made King do the seven-11 thing, and there was a seat. We sat down and watched the movie.

"Chicago beat us that night. Never again did Imlach invite me to go to a show, never. It was like the whole thing never happened."

Through the 1960s, the train remained the primary method of travel in the six-team NHL. Teams might fly by airplane in the playoffs when they wanted to get home quickly and rest but during the regular season the train remained king.

"When we went by train, both with Day and Smythe and Imlach and Clancy, we had a Pullman car with 12 lower berths and 12 uppers," Haggert said. "At end of the car was a stateroom with upper and lower berths, but it had a door. That gave Imlach and Clancy their own little room.

"Once they shut their door, you could do whatever you wanted. You could have a few beers. They didn't care as long as there was no trouble or you weren't getting hammered. They gave you a break."

The 24 berths in the Pullman car were assigned the same on every trip. Foster Hewitt, the legendary broadcaster who called the Leafs games on radio, had the first lower berth. The rest were assigned in order of the players seniority in the NHL.

"When Red Kelly got traded from the Detroit Red Wings to us, he'd been with the Wings for a lot of years, so he got preference," Haggert said. "Somebody got bumped to the upper row so he could have a lower berth. Kelly was treated like a proper veteran. Anytime somebody came to your team with more seniority in the league, you got bumped from the lower berth.

"Everybody knew their berths. Tommy Naylor and I got upper 23 and 24."

Foster Hewitt travelled with the Leafs for more than 30 years. Thanks to his pioneering work as the radio voice of the Maple Leafs, Hewitt was more famous across Canada than many of the players. He was also careful enough with the money he made as a broadcaster to buy his own radio station, CKFH, the FH standing for his own initials. But, Haggert says, Hewitt kept himself remote from the players.

"Foster would always get on the train on time. He'd get in his berth, pull the curtain, and you wouldn't know he was in there," Hewitt said. "And he was the first guy off in the morning. He also never stayed at our hotel. CKFH had a deal with another hotel chain, so he stayed there.

"It was weird. He'd get off the train and there'd be a bus for us to our hotel, and he would get a cab to his hotel. The next time we'd see him would be after the game. I'll bet Foster Hewitt didn't go to 15 practices in his life.

"He would come in the Wood Street entrance of the Gardens because CKFH was at Wood and Yonge [Street]. On Wednesday nights, he would come from his office. He'd walk in the Wood Street door, and Stan Obodiac, the public relations guy, would give him a piece of paper. The paper would say who's in and who's out of the lineup. There was only one piece of paper, not all the stats and stuff they have now.

"Foster never came to the dressing room. Maybe once or twice in the playoffs, he'd come in and say, 'Way to go, guys.' He never came to a practice.

"He'd take the piece of paper, go upstairs to his gondola, and say, 'Hello Canada and hockey fans in the United States.' Then he'd give the lineup changes and go to the national anthem. After the game, Hewitt would come down to the press room, which was next door to the dressing room, and then maybe go into the Hot Stove Lounge and have a beer and go home.

"You never saw him if you were a player."

Train travel, even for a group like the Maple Leafs with their private car, could be uncertain. They travelled overnight a lot, and the car could be shunted between several different trains, depending on their journey.

"If you were going to Chicago, it was all night," Haggert said. "You would get in at eight o'clock in the morning. For New York and Boston, you would go to Albany [New York] and either turn right to go to New York City or turn left to Boston.

"They'd bump our car around three or four times a night. You never knew where the hell you were. You'd get into Boston at the South Station, for some reason, and the damn game would be at the North Station [where the old Boston Garden was]. I never figured it out.

"There would be a bus to pick up the players. On a normal day, we'd be there by noon on game day, with the game at eight o'clock."

Given that most of their travel was during the winter, however, there were lots of days that were not so normal.

"I remember seven trips to Boston one year and we never made it on game-time," Haggert said. "We'd get to Albany, it would be noon and we weren't even halfway there yet. So what did we eat for our one o'clock meal?

"The train people would call ahead and put a dining car on. Someone would cook dinner, and we'd eat. Then, 50 miles down the road, they would pull that car off.

"Then, when you finally got to the station in Boston, everybody was going nuts because we were late.

"You wouldn't see daylight on the trip. From the South Station, it was on the bus to the game. Then the game's over and you went downstairs at the Boston Garden and walked to the North Station. You would get on a train again and take it all night to Montreal. Then, the day train from Montreal to Toronto got in at six o'clock on Monday night. We'd leave Toronto at midnight Saturday night, get home six o'clock Monday night, and had barely been off the train.

"You didn't know where the hell you were. Halfway through the night, going through Vermont, the customs guys would wake you up at four o'clock in the morning. You'd show them your ID. Then they would switch your car off the Vermont express on to Canadian National train.

"You wouldn't get off the train in all that. You'd go down to the dining car, they'd close it off for an hour [from the other passengers] so everybody could eat, and then you'd go back to bed. There was nothing else to do. Somehow we made it through, though. Things fell into place."

As the Leafs trainer, Haggert was a participant in one of the most famous Leafs legends: the 1964 Stanley Cup Final in which defenceman Bobby Baun scored the winning goal in overtime of the sixth game on a broken leg. This brought the Leafs back from a 3–2 deficit to tie the series against the Detroit Red Wings and force a seventh and deciding game in Toronto, which the Leafs won.

Haggert says there are some key elements to the story that have been forgotten over the years. Leafs coach Punch Imlach exploited a Red Wings faux pas before Game 6 to rouse his players and Leafs centre Red Kelly was also hurt in Game 6. No one knew until the last minute if either Baun or Kelly was going to play in the final game, and Imlach milked this to great effect.

Also, Baun himself chipped in with a sidelight—the fact he disappeared between Games 6 and 7 to the great consternation of Imlach. But more on that later.

The Detroit Olympia was big enough for the Leafs' team bus to drive inside the building, which it did, and an infuriating sight greeted the Leafs.

"We were the defending champions, but we were stumbling," Haggert said. "We were thinking, 'Hey, tonight it might be all over.'

"We got off the bus and here's this great big frigging horseshoe, the size of a wall. It was covered in red and white roses and said Detroit Red Wings, 1964 Stanley Cup Champions. They had it all ready, so if they won that night, they'd take it out on the ice.

"We had to walk by it. Not nice. The guys were really pissed off. Imlach, of course, made note of it in his pregame speech."

The Red Wings took a 3–2 lead in the second period until Leafs winger Billy Harris, who had not been on the ice, was sent out for his first shift and scored to tie the game. In the third period, the Wings hammered away at the Leafs, with goaltender Johnny Bower holding them off.

One of the Detroit shots, by centre Alex Delvecchio, hit Baun on the right leg.

"You're right, there's 30 versions of what happened after that, and I'm not sure which is the right one," Haggert said. "There's some things people have said that I don't remember happening. Anyway, here is what I remember:

"We got him off the ice, and Bobby Baun was one of the toughest human beings you will ever meet. He had a pain threshold that was just absolutely beyond belief. He'd play going through fire.

"We were also very lucky that Detroit was then the only team in the six-team league that had a portable X-ray machine in their building. Every team was required to have an infirmary that was available to both teams. The Detroit doctor had to look after both teams in the regular season.

"But when we travelled in the playoffs, our own head doctor, Dr. Jim Murray, was with us. In that series, he had a friend of his along, a doctor from Chicago named Bill Stromberg. We also had Carl Illiafe, our physiotherapist, and me and Tommy Naylor, the other assistant trainer.

"We rushed Baun down to the clinic, and they took an X-ray. The Detroit doctor brought it down to us and said, 'He's got a hairline fracture.' So there we were.

"There was King Clancy, the assistant general manager; Imlach, the coach and manager; Ballard; Stafford Smythe. There was a cast of thousands. We're all talking about what we should do—'Can he play, and if he plays, how much worse can it get? If he turns his leg or stops another shot, does this mean the end of his career? Does this mean if we win this game, can he play the seventh game? Could this be career-ending?'

"Baun had the final decision. No one was threatening him to play. Everybody was talking to everybody else—'What do you think? I don't know, what do you think?' This was going on partly around Baun in the clinic and partly out in the hall."

As for Baun, he was begging the doctors to freeze his leg so he could get back in the game. Finally, a consensus was reached.

"We decided, collectively, that since it was a hairline fracture, I could tape him up so it was damn near close to being a cast," Haggert said. "In other words, nothing was going to move. So in a minute it was, 'Let's do it.'"

Dr. Bill Stromberg, Dr. Murray's pal, gave Baun the freezing he wanted, and then he was turned over to Haggert, who had to prep him for the tape job.

"Now Baun was one of the hairiest guys you ever saw," Haggert said. "We had to shave him from his knee right to his toes. Carl Illiafe and I had that job. Then it was my job to tape him. I taped him, and I'll tell you it was better than a cast.

"So we waltzed him from the clinic to the dressing room, and we were going to play. Oh hell yes, there was no doubt he wanted to play, but we had to be very careful in case there was a compound fracture and he ended up in a cast for six months.

"That being said, nowadays you have to fill out, if someone cuts their finger, a report ten pages long. One goes to the office, one goes to the NHL, one goes to the NHLPA. In those days you could do what you wanted but not recklessly. I didn't do anything without the doctors' okay. Nobody worked on their own, saying, 'Geez, I hope it works out.'"

Baun was back in the game when it went into overtime. A few minutes into the sudden-death period, he took a shot at the Detroit net that hit defenceman Bill Gadsby and eluded goaltender Terry Sawchuk. The Leafs were alive for the deciding game, and Baun became a folk hero.

The Leafs flew into Detroit for the game because it was the playoffs, and on their flight home afterward, Baun was not the only player hurting badly. Red Kelly tore some knee ligaments during the game, and he was in more pain than Baun.

"What a lot of people never focused on was that Red Kelly was also hurt," Haggert said. "He couldn't walk. He had serious knee trouble.

"We had an ambulance meet us at the airport when we got home after the game, and it took Kelly right to the hospital. We had a day off before the seventh game. Baun was the big story, but of equal importance was Kelly. And his injury was more severe."

It is at this point that Baun picks up the story. When Haggert's recollection about the 1964 Cup final was brought up at a reunion of the Leafs' 1967 Stanley Cup team on February 18, 2007, Baun added another tidbit few people remember. Game 6 of the 1964 Cup final was played in Detroit on April 23, and the Leafs won 4–3 in overtime. Game 7 was on April 25, and Baun says Punch Imlach spent most of the day between games in a rage looking for his defenceman.

Baun said he wanted some peace and quiet in order to rest on the day off. He also did not want his family besieged by reporters and others wanting to know if he was going to play in Game 7. So he turned to a friend who owned a farm outside of Toronto.

"They had to keep freezing my leg [during both games]," Baun said. "The freezing wouldn't stay in very long. Red was the same way. He had a tough time with his ligaments, so it was very difficult. He was probably in more pain than I was.

"I kept the leg frozen for about three days after I broke it, but I wouldn't go to the hospital. I came off the plane from Detroit, and I disappeared. Punch was getting real mad because he couldn't find me. Only my wife knew where I was.

"My friend had a farm, and I went there. I knew nobody would know where I was, and I didn't want all that pressure on my family. I kept my leg on ice the whole time I was at my friend's house and just relaxed.

"No, Punch couldn't scream at me, because he didn't know where the hell I was."

Baun showed up at Maple Leaf Gardens at 6:30 in the morning on the day of the game and let the doctors take over. Whether or not he went to the hospital to join Kelly for the day remains unknown.

Haggert says Imlach rarely gets credit for being a promotional whiz, but the way he handled the situation leading up to the opening faceoff on April 25, 1964, was the mark of a genius.

"It was amazing how Imlach orchestrated everything," Haggert said. "In Maple Leaf Gardens, the visiting team dressed right across the hall from the home team. They had a buzzer in each dressing room. It went off when it was time for the teams to go on the ice.

"Imlach had given his speech before the game and then we brought Kelly and Baun in through the back door to the Gardens. Nobody knew they were there. Nobody knew where they were all day. The excitement in the building was really starting to build—'Are they playing, are they not playing?' I can remember it like yesterday.

"The Red Wings knew Baun was hurt, and they probably knew Kelly was hurt, because it had been written about. He wasn't at the practice the day before. The buzzer went off, but Imlach held our team back. I got up to open the door, and Imlach said, 'Shut that door and get in here. Let them go on the ice first.'

"Detroit went on the ice, and they were skating around, shooting pucks. But there were no Toronto Maple Leafs. Everybody in the stands was on their feet. They were all yelling, 'Go Leafs, Go!' but there were no Leafs. Imlach orchestrated this so well.

"Then the referee came and banged on the door. I answered the door, He said, 'Haggert, tell Imlach to get the team out here in 15 seconds or I'll charge you a delay-of-game penalty. Imlach argued for a second and then said okay.

"So out came the Leafs team, and Imlach kept Kelly and Baun in the dressing room. They were ready to go. They had novocaine; they were taped up; you name it, it was done. The Leafs went on the ice, and the Detroit guys were skating around, asking, 'Where's Baun? Where's Kelly?' and they were puffing up their chests.

"Now the fans caught on, and they were getting louder and louder. Imlach turned to me and said, 'Let Kelly out.' Kelly went out, and wow, there was a two-, three-minute ovation. Then he told me to send Baun out. I never heard an ovation like that. And Imlach orchestrated that like it was theatre.

"When Baun stepped on the ice, I looked over at the Detroit guys. Honest to God, their heads dropped right down. I said to Punch when he came behind the bench, 'Punch, you haven't got a worry in the world. We're going to win easy tonight.'

"It was pure brilliance. The ovations Kelly and Baun got took our team to another height. And it took the air right out of the Detroit guys. And we won. We didn't win easy, but we won."

The record shows the Maple Leafs won the game 4–0 to grab their third consecutive Stanley Cup. Andy Bathgate scored early in the first period, and the Leafs clung to that 1–0 lead until late in the third period when they scored three times. Kelly was one of the goal scorers, and he went from the game back to the hospital.

"Imlach set them up and knocked them down," Haggert said.

3

McKENNY'S MISADVENTURES

Jim McKenny was a fun-loving, free-skating defenceman who admits he had no hope of sticking with a disciplinarian like Leafs GM and head coach Punch Imlach. He earned his nickname Howie because of a resemblance to legendary NHL carouser Howie Young.

McKenny graduated from the Leafs' junior team, the Toronto Marlboros, after the 1965-66 season, but Imlach wanted no part of a teenage defenceman who loved to rush the puck. McKenny spent the next five seasons playing a handful of games with the Leafs and bouncing around the Leafs' minor-league chain with stops in Tulsa, Rochester, and Vancouver.

It was not until Imlach was fired after the 1969 playoffs that McKenny found a place on the Leafs. He spent the next eight-plus seasons with the Leafs, then went back to the minors after the arrival of another defensive guru, Roger Neilson.

When his hockey career was over, McKenny put his gift for gab to work and got into broadcasting. After a stint in radio, McKenny went to CITY-TV in Toronto in the mid-1980s and is still there, still telling stories, still married to his wife of forty years, Christine.

Well, one thing is different. McKenny admits many of his off-ice antics were fuelled by his addiction to alcohol. But McKenny has been clean and sober since his playing days ended and serves part-time as a drug and alcohol counselor.

McKenny says there was never a chance he could coexist with Imlach. His love for going coast to coast with the puck was bad enough. Throw in his adventures off the ice, and Imlach wanted no part of him. He was sent to the Tulsa Oilers of the Central Hockey League for most of the 1966-67 season, and then the Leafs moved him to the Rochester Americans in the American Hockey League. He also got in half a dozen games with the Leafs, which were not enough to be considered an official member of Toronto's last Stanley Cup winner.

"Oh, it was terrible," McKenny said. "I was gone as soon as I was there. But I went to camp in terrible shape. I was 210 pounds, and I had no idea how to play. I could do whatever I wanted in junior. I always carried the puck.

"But when I got to pro, I found out you couldn't do that. I had no idea how to carry the puck, no idea how to play. All I had was guys screaming at me. I said, 'Screw this. Get me out of there,' so they sent me to the minor leagues."

The NHL Players' Association was not a force when McKenny came out of junior hockey in the mid-1960s. Players had to accept the salary they were offered or take a chance on staying home to force a raise. Few of them did. McKenny says he got an early lesson on hockey economics as a junior player when an Ontario Hockey League all-star team played the national team from the old Soviet Union.

"We had Bobby Orr and Mickey Redmond on our team, guys like that," McKenny said. "We played the big Russian team at the Gardens, and there were 15,000 people there. I think it ended up in a six-all tie. We had the lead, but Derek Sanderson took a penalty near the end of the game, the Russians got a power play and tied it up.

"When the game was over, we all got Samsonite suitcases. They probably cost 16 bucks each, but we were all thrilled just to get a chance to play. The

Gardens must have made two or three hundred thousand dollars that night."

When McKenny landed in Rochester, the Americans were run by Joe Crozier, a close friend of Imlach who would later coach the Buffalo Sabres and the Leafs. He was a typically tight-fisted minor-league operator, as McKenny soon discovered.

The Americans were short a trainer because one of them had to quit suddenly to tend to his ailing wife. Crozier decided to fill the vacancy with extras from the playing roster.

"I broke my ankle, so I became the trainer," McKenny said. "Whoever was handy had to be the trainer because Cro wasn't going to hire someone sight unseen if he could get some stiff from the players.

"So I had to do all that crap, wash the floor, do all that with a cast on my leg. But it was still fun. You didn't give a shit when you were young. You were still part of the team.

"The guys would give you a hard time. They'd call you service man, and you had to get them all their stuff."

Don (Grapes) Cherry went on to coach the Boston Bruins in the 1970s, and then his fame and wealth exploded when he later became a commentator on CBC Television's *Hockey Night in Canada*. But in the late '60s, he was a down-trodden minor-league defenceman and McKenny's mentor in Rochester.

"I was there from 1966 to 1969, more or less, and I roomed with Grapes," McKenny said. "He was sort of a whipping boy for Crozier. Crozier would always get on his ass. Then Grapes would get pissed off and the guys would laugh about it. He would always complain the other guys were getting a better deal than him, and they were. Cro was screwing him on his contract. Well, we all were getting screwed, actually."

Even the players in the NHL were getting shortchanged by the owners.

McKenny would practice with the Leafs now and again when he was a junior player with the Marlboros, and he quickly learned of the disparities in pay. The best players were not always the best paid if they were not also the best negotiators.

"When Johnny Bower was a Leaf, the most he ever made when Punch was GM was 26 grand [a year]," McKenny said. "That would be okay if that was what everybody was getting, but then Andy Bathgate came over from the New York Rangers, and he was making 38 grand. He was making 12 thousand more than Bower. That's 50 per cent more, and his team was never even in the playoffs.

"The money was bad in the NHL, but it was really bad in the minors. You were lucky to make 3,000, maybe 3,200. Thank God for all those hockey-card collectors. A lot of guys think they're a pain in the ass, but they're supporting guys like Bobby Hull and any Hall of Famer. If they go to those card shows, they can make three or four grand in an hour. Bower makes more now signing cards than he used to when he was playing."

The reason he would practice with the Leafs as a junior player, McKenny said, was because he was regularly suspended from high school for various misdeeds. One benefit was that he got to know Johnny Bower, who shared the goaltending with Terry Sawchuk.

"Whenever I was kicked out of school, which was quite often, I had to practice with the Leafs to keep me out of trouble," McKenny said. "They used to practice at the Tam O'Shanter rink up in Scarborough because it was close to where Punch lived. That place was a hole. It was freezing cold.

"Bower and Sawchuk would skate around before practice," McKenny said. "Sawchuk would skate all day if you let him, because he didn't want to practice. Imlach would tell him to get in the net, so he'd stand there waving at the puck, going, 'Nice shot.' Then he'd turn it up and you couldn't get a pea by him. Bower would skate twice around the ice and then go in the net.

"Johnny Bower was the nicest guy you will ever meet. He was pretty easygoing and hardly ever got mad. But one day, the guys were all scoring on Bower like crazy. They were all laughing, saying, 'You're a sieve.' Bower didn't say anything, just showered and left. He was really pissed off.

"The next day at practice they had about one thousand shots on Bower. Only three went in and one of them just trickled in. Bower goes off the ice, showered, dressed, and started to leave. He got to the door, turned around and said, 'Fuck you,' and left. The guys were laughing so hard they were crying."

Another veteran the teenage McKenny got to know was Leafs captain George (Chief) Armstrong. Like most athletes, the Leafs thought someone else's pain was hilarious, and Armstrong provided some laughs in that regard during the preseason schedule.

"We played an exhibition game out in Vancouver because the Leafs owned the Victoria team and had an interest in the Vancouver team [in the Western Hockey League]," McKenny said. "Chief blocked a shot, and in those days you didn't fall down on the ice when you got hurt. If it at all possible you got off on your own steam. You didn't want to show the other team you were hurt.

"So Chief is trying to get off on one leg. He's paddling with his stick across the ice and sliding on one leg. Vancouver had this little guy, Gordie Vejprava. He was about 5-foot-2 and 150 pounds. Vejprava is coming along the boards and didn't see Chief. He ran into him and knocked him flying. The whole bench is roaring laughing, and Chief is still swimming on the ice, yelling his head off."

Armstrong and Bower were close friends, and Armstrong had a favourite trick he would pull on Bower when the team was on the road. According to McKenny, Bower would fall for it every time.

"They'd go to a department store after the pregame meal, just to kill some time before their nap," McKenny said. "Chief would always get Bower to go by the lingerie section. Chief would say he had to get something for his wife. Johnny would be embarrassed, but he'd go.

"Then Chief would hide on him, leave Bower standing there. All the other guys would be there watching, and Johnny would be so embarrassed. Chief would do it all the time to him."

In one of his first seasons with the Leafs, McKenny was roommates with Armstrong. It wasn't much fun, he recalls, and not because Armstrong was one of the oldest players on the team and McKenny was a rookie.

"Chief slept in a toque," McKenny said. "He liked having fresh air in the room, so he'd have the windows wide open. The snow would be in the room, and he's lying there with the covers pulled up to his chin and his toque down over his face.

"I'd be out all night, so he knew I'd be the first one up to have a leak. I'd get up, and there's Chief with his toque on. He would always say, 'You want to get that window?' I'd close the window, and he would wait until the room was warm, and then he'd get out of bed. Then we would go to practice.

"Chief was really cheap, so one time I said, 'I bet you don't have the windows open at home.' He said, 'No, I got them nailed shut.'"

Armstrong was, as McKenny said, careful with his money.

"All his signing bonuses and any other extra money he had, he put in Maple Leaf Gardens stock, which kept doubling," McKenny said. "He also owned a hotel in Hamilton, which did well. He never lived beyond his means. He still lives in same house he always did."

It made sense, then, not long after retiring as a player, to call Armstrong when McKenny had to make a career decision.

"Chief is a really good businessman, and I was in a jam," McKenny said. "I was selling programs [to television and radio stations]. I made one sale in a year and a half, and that program turned out to be already sold, so I had to call the guy up and say it was gone. I knew this was not going to work out.

"One of my clients was Q-107 radio, so I had a chance to go there, do radio broadcasts, and be in sales. I also knew a computer guy who was looking for somebody to work in a new company that was starting up.

"I phoned Chief and asked what I should do. He said, 'I don't know

Leaf captain George Armstrong (left), who is giving Andy Bathgate a drink from the Stanley Cup, is a careful man with money.

about these computers. I'd go with the radio job, at least that's going to be around for a while. So I took the Q-107 job.

"The computer company turned out to be Nortel. The guy who took my spot with Nortel, I think he owns his own island now down in the Bahamas. He made ten, 15 million dollars in the next five years."

All things considered, though, McKenny knows he and Armstrong made the right decision.

"Oh, yeah, I had a much better time," he said. "It was perfect for me."

Veteran players in the 1960s thought the off-season was a time for a summer job, with golf and beer drinking as their main recreation. Not many had the time or the inclination to work out to stay in shape for training camp. Armstrong and the other Leafs veterans were no exception.

"He never trained in the summer," McKenny said. "But a week before training camp, Chief would skate with us at the Gardens so his feet didn't get sore at training camp. After the practice, Chief would have a sauna.

"There was a full-length mirror in the dressing room, and when he came out of the sauna, Chief would stand in front of it. He had a big pot on him by then, and his arms were like sticks. But he was very strong. You never saw anybody lift his stick.

"He'd be in front of the mirror—he'd have his teeth out, and he'd say, 'Oh, you're beautiful.'"

In training camp, Armstrong had a strict routine in the sauna, and he did not like his teammates interfering. If they did come in the sauna while he was in it, Armstrong had a unique way of responding, although McKenny said this had some unusual repercussions on one occasion.

"After practice, he always in the sauna," McKenny said. "He would stay until he had one hundred drips of sweat come down. It was a weight control thing with him.

"Every day it was getting more and more crowded in the sauna. Chief would tell [trainer] Joe Sgro to keep the guys out of there because he needed the sauna to get himself ready for the season.

"One day, I guess the boys were out drinking the night before, so they were all in there when Chief went in. He couldn't get a seat, so he pissed on the [sauna] rocks. He thought it would clear a couple of seats for him. Well, it did, but it stunk out not only the sauna but the whole dressing room. It also wrecked the rocks.

"They had to replace the rocks. Chief was a little embarrassed because he didn't think it would have that kind of effect. So he told Joe Sgro he would look after getting new rocks. Joe told him where the sauna store was, and Chief found out they wanted 50 or 60 bucks for the rocks.

"He says the hell with that and drives his car down to the Don River. He grabbed a bunch of the rocks from the river bank. He brings them in, puts them in then sauna, and tells Joe, 'I went to the sauna store, and these cost me a fortune.'

"Two days later, Ricky Ley is sitting in the sauna and the rocks started exploding. Bang! Bang! Ricky comes out of the sauna, and he's all cut to shit. The moisture in the rocks made them explode when they got hot.

"The Chief had to own up that he got the rocks down at the Don River. Geez, the guys just roared."

Armstrong, however, remembers it a little differently.

"That story just grew over the years," he said. "It's like every guy who ever played in the NHL was a great player the longer he's retired. I never replaced any rocks.

"I did pee on them, but that was just to pull a trick on the guys. You'd pee on the rocks and then hold the door shut to stink them out. The rocks never had to be replaced."

By the time he made the Leafs for good, in the 1969-70 season, McKenny had a serious drinking problem, although he wasn't aware of it. Almost all of the players had a few drinks after practices and games, which didn't help McKenny much.

"I was an alcoholic then, but I knew nothing about the disease," he said. "I thought it was really bad that I was out all the time getting hammered. I didn't realize when I started drinking I couldn't stop. I had the disease called alcoholism.

"Most guys have six beers and stop. That's enough for them. But I couldn't stop. The mental aspect of it was hard too. You'd end up getting hammered for 40 days in a row and you'd still play. Well, that ain't easy."

Nowadays, McKenny works part-time as a drug and alcohol counselor and says, "It's the best part of my life."

It's also different around the NHL these days too. Since the million-dollar contracts came along in the early 1990s, not many players spend all of their leisure time in bars.

"Yeah, exactly, guys know they have to stay in shape to keep the money coming in," McKenny said. "It was party hearty all the time when I was in the NHL. You couldn't wait to go on the road.

"If it was a six o'clock flight, you would be at the airport at one. 'Yeah, honey,' you'd tell your wife, 'it's an early flight.'

Given the nocturnal habits of the players, curfews were enforced more vigorously in McKenny's day than they are now. Actually, he says, the players preferred an early curfew for logistical reasons.

"You wanted to have the curfew early so you could sneak back out of the hotel before closing time," McKenny said. "It was better if the curfew was at 11 o'clock, not 12. You'd all be at the bar and someone would say, 'Anybody going back?' 'Naw, let them get us all, screw 'em.' It was better to be in shit together.

"If it was just one or two guys out, you would be in shit. But if there were 20 of you out, they might not do anything. If you found out they were checking rooms, you would usually go back.

"Someone would go back early and see. Then he'd call the bar and let us know. He'd say, 'They're checking. Tell the guys to get their asses back here.' If you were five minutes late getting back, you could say I was with my uncle from Latoque or something."

The team hotel was never far away for a simple reason. No one made enough money to want to spend it on taxis. The players did not dip into their own funds until their modest meal money was used up.

"Most of the spots we liked were within walking distance of the hotel," McKenny said. "You didn't have extra money for cabs because you only got about eight bucks a day for meal money, maybe 12."

The meal money was dispensed before a road trip by traveling secretary Howie Starkman, who carried a bag of cash for the purpose. Players liked the longer trips because that meant a bigger wad of cash up front.

"No one had credit cards back then," McKenny said. "It was all cash. If you were going on the road for five days, you would get a hundred bucks or whatever, that was large. But when you were tapped out, you needed the other guys."

Players could also go back to Starkman and get a cash loan that would be paid back with a deduction on their next pay cheque. Starkman, in addition to his other duties, had to keep a running tally of who owed what.

"Howie Starkman always carried the cash, so Howie was always very popular," McKenny said. "The first guy who got to him could get two, three hundred bucks and then you were flush again. But after four days on the road, Howie would be getting pretty thin too.

"It was a total pain in the ass for Howie, all the paperwork. He would give the money out to the guys, then have to tell payroll, 'Take three hundred off his cheque, two hundred off his.' But Howie would always do it."

Howie was especially popular when the boys were playing cards on the team flights.

"We'd be back in the card game, yelling, 'Howie, get that money back here,'" McKenny said. "He'd come back, and he'd be giving out the meal money. Then he'd get in the game and lose a hundred or two."

McKenny said Starkman was always careful to add himself to the list of debtors when he made his report to the payroll department at the end of a trip.

The most popular card game on the planes was called "Stuke". It was a form of blackjack where the players took turns dealing and the dealer put up the pot, usually $200. Then each player would try to beat the dealer in turn, with the dealer keeping the pot once he had played everyone in the game twice. The players could bet any amount against the dealer's hand, right up to the entire pot. If someone won the pot, the game would move to a new dealer.

"Sometimes, there would be $1,400 or $1,500 in the pot the second time through the guys," McKenny said. "This was all on commercial flights too. We'd be yelling and swearing and drinking. This was a lot of money for us."

Ian Turnbull was a relatively well-paid young defenceman who did not spend much time worrying about finances. He would do the same thing every time the dealer came to him.

"Ian Turnbull would always go for the pot," McKenny said. "He'd be sitting back there having a few cocktails and we'd say, 'Bull, you're up.'

"'How much is in there?' he'd say. You'd always have to count it up. You'd say, 'Twelve hundred,' and he'd say, 'Pot.' He'd go pot all the time. It didn't matter how much was in there.

"Sometimes he'd lose three or four thousand dollars, and sometimes he'd win. He didn't give a shit."

Turnbull wasn't the only one who lived in the moment. And why not? Life was pretty good if you were young and on the Maple Leafs.

"The guys loved playing cards," McKenny said. "It was all life and death, all seventh game of the Stanley Cup when you were playing cards with a bunch of athletes.

"It was fun all the time. You were traveling around with 24 of your best buddies for 15 years, with money. Your only responsibility was making the bus on time."

One thing about Leaf owner Harold Ballard was that he could be churlish in the extreme to his employees, but the players generally escaped that treatment. He also did away with almost all of the traditions established by Conn Smythe. But like many an old-fashioned boss, Ballard would step in if one of his employees had a problem.

"If you were ever in trouble, Ballard would help you," McKenny said. "But I know he was never a big fan of mine. When I was finished [as a player], I used to train on my bike in High Park. He'd come up here with his dog, Puck, and with Henry, his driver. He'd bring the dog up to the park for a run.

"I'd be riding around on my bike, see him sitting there, and yell, 'Fuck off, you old prick!' Then I'd go around the circuit again and yell again. He couldn't see it was me, and he'd be yelling, 'Who the fuck are you?'

"I wouldn't say anything and go around a few more times. Then I'd stop, and he'd laugh like hell. He loved it. He was great that way, but he was crazy."

Most Leafs fans of a certain age will tell you the biggest trade in the late 1960s or early 1970s was the one that sent star winger Frank Mahovlich, Pete Stemkowski, Garry Unger, and the rights to Carl Brewer to the Detroit Red Wings for Norm Ullman, Paul Henderson, and Floyd Smith on March 3, 1968. McKenny disagrees. He says his favourite Leaf trade of that era came on November 29, 1973, when the Leafs sent Pierre Jarry to the Red Wings for Tim Ecclestone.

"Pierre Jarry was a great guy, and he was my roomie," McKenny said. "But Ecclestone was beautiful. He was one of the funniest guys I ever played with. He was a fringe player, but he didn't give a shit about anything."

McKenny even managed to laugh when he, an avowed pacifist, was set up by Ecclestone for a long night with Dave (The Hammer) Schultz and the rest of the brawlers on the Philadelphia Flyers of the 1970s.

"In Philadelphia, it was always a real pressure situation," McKenny said. "One night there, the game was just starting, and Dave Schultz skates by our bench. Ecclestone yells, 'Hey Hammer, if I get out there tonight, I'm gonna kick your ass.'

"I'm roaring laughing, and Schultzie looks at our bench. I look at Ecclestone, who was sitting beside me. He's got his head down, pretending to tie his skates. Schultz looks right at me, and now he thinks it was me.

"He chased me around for two periods until I finally told him it was Ecclestone, not me."

Inge Hammarstrom and Borje Salming were among the first Swedes to play in the NHL regularly and the first to play for the Leafs. Harold Ballard always complained because Hammarstrom, a highly skilled forward, did not care for the rough stuff. One of the Leafs owner's most famous quotes was that Hammarstrom could go into a corner with six eggs in his pocket and not break any of them.

"If Inge Hammarstrom was playing now, he'd be a 75-goal scorer," McKenny said. "There wouldn't be anybody slashing or holding him. He had so much talent, but it was so crude back then you could kill a guy and it would be a five-minute penalty.

"We were happy Ballard said it about him because there were about four or five of us in the same boat. But Harold was focused on poor Inge.

"One time there were guys bleeding all over the bench, and Ecclestone leaned over to Inge and said, 'I bet this wasn't in the brochure, eh?'"

John F. Bassett was the son of John Bassett, the Leafs chairman. Johnny F, as the younger Bassett was called, was a hip young fellow who tried his hand at various ventures, including upstart hockey and football leagues. He owned the Toronto Toros of the World Hockey Association and the Memphis Southmen, who started out as the Toronto Northmen, in the World Football League during its brief existence.

Before getting into sports, Johnny Bassett went into the movie business. In 1971, he was the producer of *Face-Off*, which was based on a book by well-known sports writer Scott Young. It was the story of an unlikely and ultimately tragic love affair between a young hockey player, Billy Duke, and a hippie pop singer. Yes, this was as turgid as it sounds, although *Face-Off* remains a cult classic among hockey fans. Its status is not as exalted as the greatest sports film ever made, *Slap Shot*, but there is much affection for it among Leafs fans because many of their heroes had speaking or walk-on parts.

George Armstrong had the biggest speaking role among the players, playing himself, as did Derek Sanderson, then a rising bad-boy star with the Boston Bruins. Harold Ballard did a turn as the team doctor and several sports writers of the day, including Young, appeared as the press entourage.

McKenny was not one of the players who had a speaking part, but when the project started, he was in the running for the lead role.

"I did three or four screen tests for it," he said. "John Bassett paid for me to go to acting school. I went to acting school for about six months, then I did the screen test. I was so bad they had to get another guy to do it."

The other guy was a young actor named Art Hindle, who was in McKenny's acting class.

"Art bullshitted them," McKenny said. "He told them he could play hockey. He'd never been on skates in his life. He played a little football, but he never played hockey. We sort of taught him how to skate. Well, it was just how to put the skates on. All of the on-ice stuff were just tight shots of him."

It was a nice move by Hindle, who went on to a good acting career. Another notable in the cast was John Vernon, who played the coach and later became famous for playing Dean Wormer in *Animal House*. McKenny had to settle for being Hindle's stand-in on the ice, which is how Billy Duke came to wear No. 18, McKenny's number.

The movie was shot in Toronto, and one of the reasons it remains a cult classic, aside from its '70s look with all the sideburns, is that much of it was shot at Maple Leaf Gardens. There is a lot of footage of NHL games cut into the action.

The funny thing is, McKenny never saw the movie when it was finished. All he saw was what was filmed when he was around.

"Chief was pretty good, I thought, compared to me," McKenny said. "He got a speaking part. I was the skating guy. No, I've never seen it.

"That film crew went with us on one of our road trips during the season. They were out drinking and partying with us. We started out in Philadelphia, went to L.A., then Oakland, and finished in Detroit. By Detroit, everyone in that film crew was in bed sick. They couldn't keep up with us. It wasn't even close. And they didn't even have to play the games, for crying out loud."

Even though he missed out on a big role, McKenny loved being part of the movie because he got to run around with Derek (Turk) Sanderson, whose reputation as a partier dwarfed his own, during the summer filming.

"I know Chief got extra money for that movie, probably 150 bucks," McKenny said. "I don't think I got shit out of it, except the acting lessons were free. But I did get to hang around with Turk.

"Once they had a day off, so they had a golf day at a course where John F. Bassett was a member. I hadn't played much golf at that time, but Turk had. He had the big Wilson bag like Ken Venturi, brand new clubs, new shoes, the whole ball of wax.

"Of course, we're both blitzed when we get there about ten o'clock in the morning. They gave us caddies. I told the caddies, 'Don't worry about the balls, just make sure I've got three cold Molson Ex in that bag at all times. Turk says, 'Yeah, and I'll have Chivas, no ice.' The kids were busy running back and forth to the bar for cocktails all day.

"Turk ended up shooting 71. He was an unbelievable golfer. He'd never seen the golf course before, and it was not an easy golf course, but he was incredible. And shitfaced too.

"We were done about 2:30 in the afternoon. Turk gives the kid $20. In those days, you tipped caddies five bucks. The kid looked like he'd died and gone to heaven, but Turk says, 'What, that's not enough for you? Take these.' And he throws his golf bag and clubs at the kid and says, 'Howie, get in the car. We're out of here.'"

McKenny and Sanderson spent a lot of time in bars that summer, with Sanderson throwing his money to everyone who crossed his path.

"He spent money like crazy in the bars," McKenny said. "I asked him how much do you tip and he said, 'Twenty per cent. But if I get recognized, it's one hundred.' Well, everybody in Canada knew who he was."

Sanderson's wild ways went on for years until he drank himself out of hockey and almost out of his life. But he managed to turn his life around and got into broadcasting like McKenny, plus one other unlikely career.

"Geez, now he's a financial consultant, doing unbelievable," McKenny said. "You talk to him now and he's showing you pictures of his kids. He's been clean for more than 20 years.

"He's still golfing, but he's not as good as he was. He could have been a pro golfer. But he had two hip replacements, which kept him in bed for a year."

Another of McKenny's favourite teammates was checking forward Gary Sabourin, whose run with the team was as brief as Ecclestone's. Sabourin arrived on May 27, 1974, in a trade with the St. Louis Blues for goaltender Ed Johnston and was shipped out a little more than a year later in a trade for forward Stan Weir. While he was in Toronto, McKenny says, Sabourin kept the Leafs laughing.

"He professed to be a great outdoorsman," McKenny said. "One time he had Darryl Sittler up to his cottage near Parry Sound [Ontario]. Sabby said he was a great fisherman.

"They were supposed to go out, but it was raining, so they were having a few pops instead. Finally, Sabby says, 'What are you, a pussy? This is the best time to catch fish.' So they go out [on Georgian Bay].

"They get out there, and the engine on the boat conks out. Sabby is the master engineer, and he's back there trying to get it started. He's pulling the rope like crazy, and finally it starts. But he had the engine in gear, and the boat took off. It swung one way, and Sabby went the other way and into the water.

"By this time it was dark. When Sitt is able to get to the back of the boat and grab the engine, Sabby is out in the water. The boat is going all over the place, and when Sitt finally gets hold of the thing, he can't find Sabby. He could be half a mile away now. Finally, Sitt had the sense to turn the thing off, and all he hears is this voice: 'I'm over here, you asshole. I know you can see me.'

"Sabby's a baker now down in Chatham [in Southwestern Ontario]. He's up at two in the morning every day, baking bread. He's still a grinder, but he doesn't mind. The worse things are, the funnier he is."

One of the stories Sabourin liked to tell McKenny and the rest of the Leafs was about his days with the Blues under head coach Scotty Bowman, who was not known as a player-friendly guy.

The Blues were playing in Toronto on a Saturday night and, like many NHL players, this was as close to home as Sabourin could play. A large group of family and friends from his hometown of Parry Sound in Northern Ontario came down to the game.

"He had about ten people and got them all tickets," McKenny said. "After the game, he's out there shooting the breeze with them. Everybody else on the team got on the bus.

"Scotty says to the trainer, 'Is everybody on?' The trainer goes up and down the bus counting the players and says, 'We're missing Sabby.'

"Scotty says, 'We're missing fuck all, let's go.' So the bus takes off, Sabby comes outside and freaks out. He was a real excitable guy. 'Jesus, I'm in trouble,' he says.

"He jumped into a cab and tells the guy, 'I'll give you 25 bucks if you can get me to the airport in 15 minutes.' The cabbie takes off, they get on the Gardiner [Expressway], and they pass the bus.

"Sabby's hanging out the cab screaming, 'You assholes, you left me!' The guys on the bus were just roaring."

Darryl Sittler was the best Leafs centre and player since Dave Keon was in his prime in the 1960s. For a time in the mid-1970s, McKenny says, he was the best player in the NHL, which is difficult to dispute. It was not until Doug Gilmour came along in 1992 that the Leafs had a comparable star.

For a brief time in the mid-1970s, McKenny was moved up from defence to play on Sittler's wing. At the time, McKenny was not playing all that much, and his promotion came as a surprise.

"I was driving down to the rink that night, and I was a healthy scratch [from the lineup]," McKenny said. "I'm just going to go down to the game watch it and relax. Then I heard on the radio that Ronnie Ellis retired. I got to the rink and found out I was playing with Sitt because Ronnie retired and he didn't tell anybody right away."

While he had not expected to be put on the Leafs' top line, playing forward was nothing new for McKenny. As an offensively inclined defenceman who was prone to mishaps at his own end of the ice, McKenny had been tried at forward by various coaches over the years.

"When I was in Rochester, they started playing me on the wing so I'd improve my skating," he said. "I also played with Andy Bathgate out in Vancouver in the Western League. When I first came to Leafs, I played defence for three years, then went back and forth on the wing."

Playing with a star like Sittler, though, was a big treat.

"Sittler was by far the best player in the league," McKenny said. "That night I had four breakaways, and I hadn't had a breakaway in five years. I was ringing them off the post all night."

Alas, McKenny said, his run for glory was over quickly. Head coach Red Kelly delivered the news.

"At the morning skate a week later, Red came over and said, 'We're going to try Lanny McDonald on the right side tonight. Lanny took off from there. The rest is history, and so was I."

McDonald wore his emotions on his sleeve, McKenny said, which did not help him with the card sharks on team flights.

"On the plane one time we were playing cards, and Lanny went for a leak," McKenny said. "We were playing gin, and I had lost the last hand. So when he left, I arranged the cards and gave him a hand that was one card from gin. If you were playing cards with Lanny, you weren't allowed to look at his face because he'd light right up with a good hand. If you played poker with him, his face was always a dead giveaway.

"I gave him those cards and then dealt my own hand, and naturally I gave myself gin. Lanny comes back from the can, picks up his hand and goes, 'Holy cow!' He's showing it to all the guys and then he picks up one card and doesn't get gin. I pick up one card and had gin. He knew I screwed him over. He threw his cards all over the plane."

McKenny said the most memorable player to him was fellow defenceman Borje Salming, who came to the Maple Leafs in 1973 along with fellow

Swede Inge Hammarstrom, a skilled winger. They were the first European players to play regularly for the Leafs and were among the first of the wave of overseas players that came to the NHL in the 1970s.

Since European players, particularly Swedes, were regarded as soft, Salming was regularly subjected to all manner of muggings on the ice. He bore it all stoically, rarely fighting back, and gained the enduring love and respect of his teammates and Leafs fans.

Salming also happened to be one of the greatest defencemen in Leafs history and for a long time was considered second in the NHL only to a fellow named Bobby Orr. It did not take long for McKenny and his teammates to appreciate Salming's talents.

"He was a great natural athlete," McKenny said. "He could have been a professional tennis player, an auto racer, just about anything he wanted."

Salming's athletic ability kept him out of trouble in Sweden too, McKenny says. He was from the town of Kiruna, which is well above the Arctic Circle, where the locals are conditioned by the long hours of daylight and darkness, depending on the season, not to rush through life.

"They have mandatory military duty in Sweden, and Borje would always get in trouble because he would never wake up in time. They would toss him in the military jail. What saved him was handball, which was a big game in the military. It's where you run around with a ball and throw it in the net.

"Borje started playing European handball in the army. He never played before, but he was so good after two months that they wanted him on the national team."

This gift extended to other sports as well.

"We went to Phoenix during a western trip because we had two days off," McKenny said. "That was the first time Borje played golf, and he shot a 90. Anything he did, he was great at. It didn't matter what—any kind of game. He was really smart too, even though he never got far in school.

"He played chess and won all the time. He was never down playing cards. He always won. We'd go to [downtown Toronto] and he'd play chess with the guys in the park and win. He'd play two games at once and beat them.

"There's a Chinese game called Go [played] with marbles. It's really complicated. My brother-in-law, who graduated at the top of his law school, he got into Go. Next thing you know, he joins the Go association and figures he's really good after about a year. He's a buddy of Borje too, and shows him the game. Within two weeks, Borje was kicking his ass. He is just an amazing guy."

Many of the Swedes and Finns who play in the NHL have a taste for speed because auto rallying is a major sport in those countries. Salming was no different, and naturally he was good at it.

"When he lived in Mississauga, Borje would bring the kids from next door to practice," McKenny said. "I saw the kids in the stands one day, and they were just dead white. I said, 'Harry, what's wrong with you?'

"He says, 'We were driving in with Borje this morning, hit some water under a bridge, did a 360, and kept going.'

"The car straightened out, and Borje kept going like nothing happened. He could do that."

Salming was challenged many, many times to fight in the NHL but rarely took anyone up. He simply ignored the intimidation tactics, shrugged off the hacking and slashing, and played his game. But one day the Leafs hanging around the dressing room got a big surprise. Kurt Walker, one of the tough guys the Leafs brought to the team in the mid-1970s to combat ferocious teams like the Philadelphia Flyers, was working on the heavy bag with Salming.

"Kurt Walker was teaching Borje how to box one day in the dressing room," McKenny said. "He was teaching him about combinations. They put the gloves on and did some sparring. About two seconds in, Borje hit him with a right hand, and Kurt's eyes were watering. He just about knocked him down.

"The rest of the guys were just roaring. Borje could really fight. He just couldn't fight on skates."

Ian Turnbull was one of the most talented Leafs in McKenny's era, but his career never added up to that of a great player. He could be one of the best offensive defencemen in the NHL when the spirit moved him, but that happened less and less over his eight years with the Leafs from 1974 to 1982. But one thing that stayed constant, McKenny said, was Turnbull's appetite for fun.

"I remember one night in L.A., we were talking about drinking tequila," McKenny said. "He said, 'I can drink that stuff all night long. It doesn't bother me.' I said, 'We'll see about that.' We were sitting at the Ramada Inn, and he started drinking shots of tequila with beer. After about ten or 12 of them, he started fading away on us.

"We had to carry him back to the hotel. Geez, he was big. He was about 200 pounds, but it was a thick and heavy 200 pounds. There's about four of us lugging him back to the hotel. We were staying at the Sheraton, which was about two blocks away from the Ramada. We were missing valuable bar time to look after this guy.

"There was a big brick wall around the Sheraton, and you had to walk around it to get to the back door. We couldn't carry him through the lobby, so we figured we'd put him up on the brick wall, run around to the other side, pull him down, and save a couple hundred yards.

"We propped him up there, and he seemed settled. I mean, he was in a friggin' coma. We run around to the other side, and in the meantime he rolls over, falls off the wall and right down into the flowerbed. The mud is up to here, and he's in there face down.

"But instead of us rescuing him, we're laughing so hard he almost smothered. We finally pried him out of the mud and pulled him in the hotel. We went and got the key to his room, put him in his room on the floor, and left him there."

Turnbull was a good skater, and this tempted Leafs head coach Red Kelly to try him as a forward. Kelly would do it now and then, only Turnbull's sense of humour made him regret it.

"Turnbull thought he was Bobby Hull when he was on the wing," McKenny said. "He called himself Bobby Hockey. He would always skate with the one finger up because Bobby had broken that finger, and it was always up.

"Turnbull would always be out there skating on the ice with the finger up, looking over at the bench. Red would be looking and say, 'Get that idiot off the ice. Somebody get him off.'

"But he wouldn't come off. If Turnbull was on the far side of the ice, he'd never get off. He'd stay out there for two and a half, three minutes, doing bugger all. And Red would go crazy."

No matter how crazy Red Kelly's players made him, one thing he never did was swear. He was raised to never take the Lord's name in vain. The strongest word to pass Kelly's lips was *dang*.

"Oh yeah, he was always saying, 'That dang guy,'" McKenny said. "One time on the plane, we were playing cards. It was hot, so Lanny [McDonald] took his shirt off. One of the stewardesses complained, so Red came down the aisle and said, 'Hey you, get your shirt on, you're not on the danged farm now.' We were just roaring."

In his book *The Leafs*, author Jack Batten recounts the story of a game in which the Leafs were awful in the first period. They were so bad, Kelly could not contain himself. He went into the dressing room and said, "Dang, you guys aren't playing worth hell."

The players were so shocked there was complete silence. It was broken by McKenny, who said, "Hey look, Red, I know we're playing bad, but you don't have to swear."

When this story was related to McKenny, he said he didn't remember it. "But," he said, "it's a good one so I'll take it."

When the playoffs came along, Kelly was fond of gimmicks that would deflect the media's attention away from the players. This was especially important in the mid-1970s when the Leafs met the Philadelphia Flyers in three consecutive years. The Flyers won two consecutive Stanley Cups, in 1974 and 1975, largely by pounding the opposition into submission and then letting their skill players go to work.

The Flyers swept the Leafs in the 1975 playoffs on their way to their second Cup, and it was clear the Leafs needed to add some muscle if they hoped to compete with the Broad Street Bullies. One year later, the teams met again in the playoffs. This time, the Leafs were ready, thanks to the addition of the likes of Kurt Walker, Dave Dunn, and Dave (Tiger) Williams.

It was one of the nastiest and most memorable playoff series in NHL history. In one game at Maple Leaf Gardens, there was a bench-clearing brawl that ended with two Flyers, Don Saleski and Joe Watson, facing assault charges. Watson was charged with assaulting a police officer when his stick came down on a cop's shoulder.

Salming was regularly gored by the Flyers and was eventually beaten up by Mel Bridgman in another game. That resulted in more assault charges, as Bridgman was arrested for attacking Salming, and Bob (Mad Dog) Kelly was charged when he threw his hockey glove into the crowd, hitting an usher.

Before the series started, to take his players' minds off the impending battle, Red Kelly told the press the Leafs were going to win with pyramid power. He said pyramids gathered energy from the North Pole and sent it out through the top of the pyramid. Kelly spent a considerable sum of Harold Ballard's money installing pyramids in the Leafs dressing room and under their bench.

Yeah, that was just Red trying to get the players going," McKenny said. "We were supposed to be afraid of the Flyers, but we were pretty well as tough as they were by then."

The Leafs lost the first two games of the series in Philadelphia, then won the next two wild ones in Toronto. In Game 6, Darryl Sittler scored five goals to send the series to a seventh and deciding game. The legend of pyramid power was cemented when Sittler said he held his stick under the pyramids before the game. Pyramid power went only so far, though, as the Leafs lost the deciding game 7–3.

That playoff series is still recalled fondly by Leaf fans, although McKenny says it wasn't a lot of fun for him and his fellow pacifists. Actually, he added, he never had any fun playing the Flyers through his whole career.

"It was good for the tough guys, but for us chickenshit guys, it was terrifying," he said. "You knew within the first two minutes of the game it was going to be a Pier Six brawl and a bench-clearer."

McKenny eventually learned what the proper strategy was when a brawl broke out and the players' benches emptied.

"You had to make sure you got off the bench early or you were dealing with the worst guy on their team," he said. "You wanted to get one of their country-clubbers, like Rick MacLeish or somebody else you could handle, like Bill Barber or Bobby Clarke. Clarke couldn't fight worth a damn.

"One night I slipped getting over the bench, and Harvey Bennett was the only friggin' guy left. His job was to knock me out as quick as possible so he could jump in on all the other fights. Once one guy got loose, if any of his guys were losing, he would go over and drill the other guy to even it up.

"I'm hanging on to Harvey Bennett, but he's about 220 pounds, and he's whaling the piss out of me. Luckily, he broke one of his knuckles about a minute into it. He only had his left hand left, so I ended up hanging on to him.

"That's when I learned that lesson: make sure you get your ass over there early. You didn't want to be the first one over, but you certainly didn't want to be the last. About fourth or fifth was good, because you could get another country-clubber.

"The goalie would grab the other goalie and they'd shoot the shit along with the rest of us country-clubbers. We let the haywires go at it, the Dave Dunns, the Tigers Williamses, the Kurt Walkers. And Sittler too. Darryl Sittler could really fight, and so could Lanny McDonald."

Those Leafs teams were tough as well as talented, but they always lost their best players because Harold Ballard would not match offers from the World Hockey Association.

Leaf defenceman Ian Turnbull marched to his own drummer.

"If they kept the guys we had, guys like Ricky Ley and Jimmy Harrison, we would have had one of the toughest teams in the league," McKenny said. "We would have won four or five Stanley Cups in the '70s."

Roger Neilson replaced Red Kelly as coach in 1977. He was a young, innovative coach who came to be considered a hockey genius. Neilson quickly earned the nickname Captain Video for introducing video sessions to hockey as a teaching tool.

"Roger was a great guy," McKenny said. "He let the players pretty much run the team—guys like Sittler, McDonald, and Salming. Those guys pretty well had a free rein. It was a good working relationship. They beat the New York Islanders that year in the playoffs. After that, the Islanders won four straight Cups, and they should have won it that year."

McKenny said *they*, because he was not part of the team when the Leafs pulled off an upset of the Islanders in the 1978 Stanley Cup quarter-finals.

Neilson preached defence above all else, which meant he and McKenny were not destined to get along. McKenny's playing time dropped, and as Christmas approached in 1977, he was sent down to the Leafs' farm team, the Dallas Black Hawks.

"Oh no, I wasn't defensive at all," McKenny said. "Neither was Turnbull, but he was playing great at the time. I got called into a room.

"Jim Gregory [the GM] was going to tell me, but Roger said, 'No, no, I'll handle this.' He called me in, and I'd been there ten or 11 years, and he says, 'You're going down to Dallas.' I said, 'Fuck, Roger, it's Christmas.'

"He says, 'Nah, you're gone.' I said, 'Well, if someone gets hurt, I'm coming back up, aren't I?' and he says, 'No, you're not coming back.' I go, 'Oh, fucking beautiful.'"

McKenny caught a flight to Dallas, went to a hotel, and sat there, feeling awfully low. Here he was, back in the minor leagues at the age of 31.

"I wasn't drinking then," he said. "I remember sitting in the Holiday Inn in a corporate mall. I was sitting on the end of the bed, feeling sorry for myself. I had just talked to a friend who was saying, 'Poor you,' so I felt really bad. Then I saw my reflection in the mirror in the dark and said, 'What the hell are you crying about?'

"Two minutes later, I was down in the lobby with a double scotch in one hand and a smoke in the other. Got into a limo and went downtown, had the greatest time. I saw poor Asher [Don Ashby] in one of the bars I hit, and I hit five or six bars. He was there with his wife, feeling bad, too. I said, 'Now that we're here, we might as well have a good time.'"

Ashby, who died in a car accident in 1981, wound up being one of the better players on the team, which also had up-and-coming young NHLers like John Anderson and Mike O'Connell. Not long after McKenny arrived, the team started playing better, and when he received his first pay cheque, he discovered the difference in the U.S. and Canadian dollars brought him a raise.

"I was pissed off when I went there," McKenny said. "But I phoned Roger about two weeks later and said, 'Hey, Rog, I'm sorry I was such a prick when you sent me down. This is the best thing that ever happened to me. I'm making about ten per cent more money, it's 80 degrees, and I'm playing golf all the time.'"

The coach of the Dallas Black Hawks, a farm team that was shared by the Maple Leafs and Chicago Blackhawks, was Gerry McNamara. He went on to infamy in the 1980s as the general manager of some of Harold Ballard's worst Leafs teams. But McNamara no more wanted to coach the Black Hawks than he wanted to be GM of the Leafs. He was happy being a scout. You did not, however, say no to Harold Ballard.

"Toronto and Chicago were together on that team, so every second year, the Leafs had to supply the coach," McKenny said. "Roger Neilson was the coach before Gerry Mac, and he was supplied by Chicago. He did so well he got the Leafs job.

"So Wirtz [Chicago Blackhawks' owner Bill] calls Ballard and says, 'Listen, it's your turn to get a coach down there, and it's September, and you haven't got a coach.' So Harold looks out his office door, and the first guy to walk by was Mac. He says, 'Hey, McNamara, get in here. You're going to Dallas. You're coaching.' That's how Mac started his coaching career.

"He didn't want to coach. He had no idea how to organize a team. When I went down there, he would only play the Leafs guys. The team was split, with the Chicago guys on one side, the Leafs on the other. The first thing I did was align myself with the Chicago guys to get things together.

"Greg Hubick [a veteran defenceman] was doing most of the on-ice things, getting a system going. All Mac would do was yell at the referees and yell at this one poor kid we had, Pierre Giroux. He was not a bad hockey player, but Mac was always on his ass real bad.

"One time, Mac told him, 'You make any more mistakes, I gotta send you home. Either send you home or send you to the I.'"

The I was the International Hockey League, then regarded as a dead-end stop for those still aspiring to an NHL career. McNamara delivered this news to Giroux just before the Chicago Blackhawks sent a very important visitor to Dallas. Bobby Orr signed a large contract with the Blackhawks the previous season, but his chronic knee problems kept him sidelined for the 1977-78 season. The Blackhawks asked him to go down to Dallas to promote the team and do some scouting.

"It was Bobby Orr Night, and he was up in the press box," McKenny said. "Next thing you know, Pierre fucks up on the ice, then Mac starts in. I was sitting on the bench, Pierre came off, and Mac was all over his ass.

"Well, Pierre dropped his gloves, and he and Mac were fighting behind the bench, rolling around on the floor. We're all laughing like hell.

"We break it up, finally, by throwing Pierre out on the ice. We got a penalty for too many men on the ice. I'm sitting on the end of the bench roaring, and I look up at Bobby, and he's sitting up there steaming. That was the way Mac handled things. When he got pissed off, he wanted to fight everybody."

Giroux spent the rest of the season with the Flint Generals in the IHL, where he had 25 goals and 23 assists in 40 games. He finally made it to the NHL in the 1982-83 season with the Los Angeles Kings. But it was a brief stay—Giroux lasted six games and scored one goal.

The Dallas Black Hawks went on to make it as far as the CHL final, where they lost in seven games to the Fort Worth Texans.

The player whose presence created the roster squeeze that forced McKenny out of Toronto was centre Jimmy Jones. Roger Neilson always had someone like Jones on every team he coached, a scrappy player short on talent but long on work ethic. Jones played on Neilson's junior teams, and he spent two seasons with the Leafs. He only scored thirteen goals in those two years, but the fans loved him because of his tenacious checking.

Tenacity, McKenny says, was the most notable thing about Jones.

"Jonesie was really tough," he said. "He used to be able to get on this running machine in the dressing room and go until he passed out. If you had friends in the dressing room, you'd say, 'Jonesie, get on this thing and show them how it works.' He'd get on there, go as hard as he could for two, three minutes, and pass right out. He'd be ready to go in another five minutes, and he'd get on it again."

One of the reasons the Leafs upset the New York Islanders in the 1978 playoffs was that Jones checked their best player, Bryan Trottier, to a standstill.

"Trottier just chopped and cut him," McKenny said. "Trottier beat the shit out of him in every game, and Jonesie just kept coming back.

"Ten or fifteen years later, I was out playing golf with a bunch of guys. It was a rainout, so we're all in the clubhouse shooting the breeze. One guy was a tennis pro, and he said, 'I taught this guy who used to play for the Leafs. I could take him out on the hottest day of the year, and he'd chase balls for three or four hours. The harder it got, the better he liked it. I can't remember his name.'

"'I said, 'I'll tell you exactly who that is: Jimmy Jones.'

"He says, 'Yeah, that's the guy.'

"Jonesie was a great guy, just an amazing person. I never saw anyone as tough as he was for a little guy. He couldn't fight worth shit, but he'd fight anybody. He'd get the shit beat out of him, come out of the box, and go right at him again and take another beating. I guess he figured, 'You're going to break a hand sooner or later.'"

When his playing career finished in 1981, Jones found another career that suited his dogged nature. He became a cop in York Region, north of Toronto, and rose to detective.

McKenny's NHL career came to an end after the 1978-79 season when he put in ten games with the Minnesota North Stars, who bought his contract from the Leafs. He played in Switzerland the next season, fulfilling a wish to play near a ski resort, and then came back home, where he eventually wound up as a television broadcaster. While he was in Minnesota, his teammates told him about Wren Blair, the first GM and head coach of the North Stars when they joined the NHL in 1967.

"One night they were really playing bad and Blair storms into the dressing room," McKenny said. "Right at the end of the period, they had three goals scored on them in two minutes. Blair is going, 'You fucking cocksuckers.' Then he slips on an orange peel and slides right under the trainer's table, which was covered in towels.

"He's under there and yells, 'I know you're all laughing out there, you bunch of cocksuckers.' Guys are just roaring. They were waiting to get shit, then that happened and they all cracked up."

4

STELLICKTRICITY

The Stellick brothers, Gord and Bob, went to work for the Toronto Maple Leafs in the late 1970s when they were both students. They landed dream jobs as go-fers in the press box, running errands and delivering statistics to reporters. Both worked their way up the organization under owner Harold Ballard. Gord became GM Gerry McNamara's assistant and then got the big job himself in 1988 by the age of 30. Gord's dream job only lasted one season, though, as he resigned in the summer of 1989 after enduring Ballard's repeated threats to fire him, delivered through columns of his favorite journalist, *Toronto Star*'s Milt Dunnell.

On August 11, 1989, Stellick walked into Ballard's office and told the owner he was finished. Ballard was quite surprised but did not try to talk him out of it.

"I thought public floggings were banned in this country," Stellick told reporters the next day. "It wasn't my team anymore. It was an empty feeling. I went into this job with my eyes open, but things changed."

Looking back on his time with the Leafs, having moved on to a career in radio and television, Stellick remembers a lot of good times even though there was a lot of bad hockey played at Maple Leaf Gardens in those years.

One of the first stories Gord remembers hearing around the Gardens concerned the cancellation of the players' annual trip to

Florida during a break in the schedule.

"The Leafs used to have a three-day sojourn to Florida back in the '70s," Stellick said. "It got cancelled because Borje Salming and Randy Carlyle were chasing each other in golf carts, *Rat Patrol* style. They were kind of bored on the golf course and were fooling around.

"Carlyle's cart hit a bump and flipped over. He got a cut and had to get about 30 stitches. He missed a few games, so that was the end of the Florida trips."

Carlyle went on to win the Norris Trophy as the NHL's best defenceman, albeit after he was traded to the Winnipeg Jets. He also won the Stanley Cup in 2007 as head coach of the Anaheim Ducks.

When Gord started with the Leafs, Punch Imlach was in his second go-round as Leaf GM. Imlach was the architect of the great Leaf teams in the 1960s and built the Buffalo Sabres from an expansion team to a Stanley Cup contender in the 1970s. But his second tour with the Leafs went badly because Imlach's dictatorial style no longer went well with the modern hockey player.

No player was more modern at the time than defenceman Ian Turnbull. He was a supremely talented player and marched to the beat of his own drummer. Imlach was no match for Turnbull's tactics when was looking for a new contract.

"When Punch came to the team [in June 1979], one of the first guys to befriend him was Turnbull," Stellick said. "Punch figured he would be one of his allies."

Turnbull cozied up to Imlach that summer long enough to get a five-year contract for about $200,000 per year. Then he stopped coming around Imlach's office.

"I don't think he ever spoke to Punch again," Stellick said. "But Punch would never acknowledge he conned him."

Turnbull was equally hard on Imlach's choice of coach, Punch's old pal

Joe Crozier. Nothing Crozier tried could motivate Turnbull.

"Joe decided to make Ian his pet project," Stellick said. "He said, 'Everybody's talking about Borje Salming, but you're my guy.' Joe decided to challenge him in a fun way about the 25 extra pounds he was carrying.

"Joe said, 'I just made a bet with Duffy [scout Dick Duff], 50 bucks, that you're going to lose those 25 pounds.' Turnbull said, 'Joe, you're going to die a poor man.'"

That was not the worst indignity Turnbull committed against Crozier. Not long before Harold Ballard fired Crozier in January 1981, the coach tried in vain to air out his indifferent troops.

"Joe Crozier was giving his last dressing room tirade, days before he got fired," Stellick said. "He was letting it all out, saying, 'I may be going down, but I'm going to take some of you guys with me,' or things like, 'Our paths will cross again.'

"Turnbull was sitting there, completely disinterested. After a while, he even lifted a cheek and let out a huge fart. It just stopped Joe. He just shook his head because there was nothing he could do."

Imlach never really accepted the entry of player agents into the hockey business. His most famous feud was with the first prominent hockey agent, Alan Eagleson, who went on to infamy himself by stealing money from the players in his capacity as head of their union.

But by his second term as Leaf GM, Imlach grudgingly came to accept agents as a necessary evil.

"In my first meeting with them together, Eagleson came in to do the Robert Picard and Rocky Saganiuk contracts," Stellick said. "It was after Punch's heart attack [in August 1980]. By that point, Eagle was so quick to get contracts done there wasn't a lot of negotiation.

"Punch put his heart medication on the table. He said to Eagle, 'I'm ready for you, you fucking prick, I got all my heart medicine right here.' Then he laughed and they signed the contracts.

"But Eagleson always said he told Punch he would piss on his grave. And he did, according to Eagleson, anyway. He's told me that a couple of times."

Harold Ballard loved publicity, and he loved to court it through his favourite writer, *Toronto Star* columnist Milt Dunnell. Gord Stellick knew for sure he was going to be the next Leafs GM when he read it in Dunnell's column in 1988, just as he knew it was all over a year later in the same fashion. He learned how this worked back in September 1981, when Punch Imlach needed a bypass operation just one year after he suffered a heart attack, his second after the one in 1972, when he was with the Buffalo Sabres.

"On our first full day of training camp, I find out Punch had to go to the hospital the night before," Stellick said. "Harold says we've got to keep this quiet. Of course, by then Harold had called Milt Dunnell. On the front page of the *Toronto Star* there's a picture of Punch in an ambulance with an oxygen mask on, being wheeled in to the hospital."

By the time Imlach's heart problems laid him out, Ballard was tired of him as the GM. This gave the owner the excuse he was looking for to get rid of Imlach.

"Harold would say, 'I don't want to put him in a box,'" Stellick said. "That was his whole thing as it went on. Harold told us to have no contact with him."

Ballard did not talk to Imlach while he was recovering. In November 1981, Imlach wanted to come back to work and called Ballard. The owner told him it would be too stressful to be general manager, so he should become a consultant. Imlach brushed this aside but soon found out Ballard didn't even want him giving advice. Mind you, Ballard didn't have the courage to tell him face to face.

"When Punch came back, he thought he was GM, but kind of knew he wasn't," Stellick said. "I think he had a sense he was going to be fired because no one was talking to him. But he made it clear, 'I'm showing up on such and such a date. I'm ready to resume action.'

"So Harold disappeared to the cottage. By then, Punch's parking spot [at Maple Leaf Gardens] was taken away. I had it. I didn't have my name up yet, but they took Punch's sign down. Punch saw that, and then he came up to the office, tried his private line and it was disconnected.

"He finally talked to Harold, who used the old 'I don't want to put you in a box,' thing. So Punch settled his expenses and he left.

"Oh yeah, in certain things Harold didn't have a lot of balls. But in others he had no problem telling you to get lost."

The front office at Maple Leaf Gardens under Ballard was like that of no other NHL team. After his wife died, Ballard had an apartment built at the Gardens and moved in. With the owner around night and day, it became a place of odd relationships between Ballard and some of his lower-level employees, who came to have some influence.

"We barely squeaked into the 1981 playoffs, and we had to play the New York Islanders," Stellick said. "This was like lambs being led to slaughter. We opened the series on Long Island with two games, back to back. The night before the first game, [head coach] Mike Nykoluk takes the team to dinner. That was pretty novel back then.

"Next thing you know, guys are ordering shooters, cigarettes, and the bill is being run up stupidly. Not by everybody, but a certain faction did. We just got creamed in those two games.

"For game three, we're back in Toronto, and Nykoluk told me to get the guys in the Westbury Hotel and have dinner at the Hot Stove Lounge [in the Gardens] after the morning skate before the game. I talked to the Hot Stove chef about getting some pasta for the meal. 'Well,' he says, 'we don't make pasta, it's all steaks,' and he's pissed off.

"I came in for the morning skate, and I cut through the kitchen like I used to do, and I saw the chef sitting in the Hot Stove Lounge with

Harold. Harold says, 'Gordie,' and gives me the finger to come over. He says, 'What the hell is this? You playing big shot in my restaurant?'

"I say, 'I don't know what you're talking about.' He says it's about ordering pasta. The chef had complained to Harold. Cripes, as the guy who ran the Hot Stove said later, all he had to do was go order Catelli spaghetti and throw it in a pot. Instead, he complains to Harold.

"Harold goes on to say you're doing a good job, but don't play the big shot in my restaurant. Miraculously, they came up with the spaghetti.

"Of course, we got smoked that night and were out in three straight games. Geez, we're at the brink of elimination, and all that was gnawing at the chef for two days was that he didn't do pasta."

One note about those Hot Stove Lounge steaks—they were delivered to your table with a small plastic cow on top. The colour of the cow determined how your steak was done.

"If you said you didn't order it medium well, they would take the steak back to the kitchen, change the colour of the cow and give it back to you," Stellick said. "They'd say it was medium rare now. It was the same steak with a different coloured plastic cow."

One of the more embarrassing incidents Stellick remembers was in November 1985, when Claire Alexander, the coach of the Leafs' farm team, the St. Catharines Saints, refused a promotion to the Leafs. The mess started when the Leafs head coach, Dan Maloney, was not allowed to hire the assistant coach of his choice. Former Leafs coach Floyd Smith was still working in the team's front office, and he had enough clout with GM Gerry McNamara to thwart Maloney's choice, his former teammate Walt McKechnie.

"Danny wanted to hire Walt McKechnie as his assistant, but Floyd was not happy about it," Stellick said. "He wasn't a big Maloney and McKechnie fan from his time as head coach. One time in Boston [when Smith was coach] they got left behind because he claimed they hid a videotape or something.

"So they assigned John Brophy as Maloney's guy. They had a year together, and the next year, '85-86, the team got off to a terrible start, and 11 games into the season, they decided to make a flip. They sent Brophy to St. Catharines and called up Claire Alexander.

"Then Alexander turned it down, and Claire's wife was on the radio saying why he won't do it."

One reason was that Alexander was upset because Brophy asked to be sent to St. Catharines. He was offended because Brophy was given his job simply by asking for it. Another reason was that Alexander's wife did not want to move to Toronto.

At the time, the Leafs were on an eight-game losing streak with a record of 1-10. The St. Catharines farm team was not doing much better under Alexander. The Saints were 4-6 and coming off a 24-50-6 record in Alexander's first season as head coach in the American Hockey League.

Alexander was from the town of Orillia, Ontario, in cottage country. He had a brief career as a defenceman with the Leafs in the 1970s and was known as The Milkman for his off-season occupation. McNamara was also from Orillia, and he and Alexander were old friends, which is why Alexander got the St. Catharines job in the first place.

Naturally, the press had a field day with the situation. Alexander's refusal to join the big league was fodder for ridicule in most NHL cities.

"We had the indignity of being the only team where the American league coach won't come up," Stellick said. "I remember telling Danny on the ice about it, and Danny smashed his stick on the glass. The situation was ridiculous. Danny just wanted Brophy out of his hair."

A day later, Alexander was mollified enough to report to work with the Leafs. But he never made much of a difference in the Leafs' fortunes, as they finished the season with a 25-48-7 record and were eliminated in the first round of the playoffs. Maloney and Alexander were fired that summer.

Brophy, on the other hand, took the Saints to the AHL playoffs with a 38-37-5 record. He wound up as head coach of the Leafs when

Maloney was fired.

"Claire was in over his head in St. Catharines," Stellick said. "I remember Bill Root talking about getting sent down to St. Catharine's. He said he put on 25 pounds and had a great time, the most fun he had playing hockey.

"Once they had a beach party in the back of the bus. They brought in sand. This was just before Claire got the call to come up to the Leafs."

Alexander was hired for the 1984-85 season thanks to one of Ballard's capricious decisions. This involved Doug Carpenter, who was coaching the St. Catharines Saints and had already been denied a promotion to the Leafs a few years earlier. Punch Imlach wanted to promote him, but Ballard refused for reasons that were not entirely clear.

"The Saints were in the playoffs, and we flew to Rochester for a game seven," Stellick said. "Ballard just didn't like Carpenter's look. He said he dressed like Herb Tarlek [from *WKRP in Cincinnati*]. Ballard made the comment that he doesn't look like a coach, and that was all Gerry McNamara needed to hear. He fired Carpenter.

"Ballard really didn't have anything against Carpenter. He just wasn't his guy."

Carpenter did not fare badly, though. He was hired by the New Jersey Devils and coached them for the next four seasons. Then he was hired as the Leafs coach by Floyd Smith, who replaced Stellick as GM in 1989. Ballard was in declining health and did not object.

"Yeah, it was very strange," Stellick said. "A guy gets fired in the American league and goes to the NHL."

Brophy was one of the most colourful coaches in Leafs history. Much of the colour came from his battles with his players. Brophy pre-

---

Leafs head coach John Brophy in mid-rant.

ferred tough players and was not enamoured of those who did not like to hit or get hit. After Brophy took over for the 1986-87 season, his least favourite player quickly became forward Miroslav Frycer, a highly skilled but enigmatic Czech whose statistics did not match his potential. GM Gerry McNamara did not share Brophy's opinion, since he brought Frycer to the Leafs in a trade with the Quebec Nordiques.

"One morning on the road, I was having breakfast with Gerry McNamara," Stellick said. "Gerry was a big Frycer guy. All the Czechs [on the team] were his guys. Gerry said, 'Broph has to get through to these guys. He can't be picking on Miroslav all the time.'

"I saw Broph over in the corner. Peter Ihnacak and Frycer were having breakfast on the other side of the room. So Broph went over to Frcyer's table and told Ihnacak to get lost and sat down with Frycer.

"Gerry said, 'This is good, Broph is going to apologize for the previous night [when he blasted Frycer].' They seemed to be chatting, and then it got a little animated. Then Broph, like usual, got louder and every second word was an f-bomb. All of a sudden he stood up and yelled at me, 'Gordie, send this guy home. He's broken down. Put him on the first plane back to Toronto.'"

Frycer's off-ice antics also did not endear him to Brophy, and even McNamara was not pleased with one in particular. In February 1986, before Brophy became coach, Frycer was charged early one morning with impaired driving. It was his second offence, and he did not tell the Leafs. They found out because a woman who worked in the Maple Leaf Gardens box office was married to a police officer.

"She phoned over during practice and said Frycer got busted for drunk driving and spent the night in jail," Stellick said. "We said, 'Are you sure?' So she called back and cited the arrest report.

"Gerry went down to practice and said, 'Mirko, anything happen last night?' So he was caught. The guy spent the night in the drunk tank and came to practice, no problem. He never cared."

Frycer wound up serving two weeks in jail.

The Frycer problem was not solved until Stellick replaced McNamara as GM.

"One of the things Broph and I agreed on was Frycer had to go," Stellick said. "So we traded him to Detroit for Darren Veitch when the season ended. About a month later, I walked into Gardens one morning, and there is Frycer looking for the trainer. He wanted to get his equipment.

"I said, 'I'll take you in.' Broph was there and came out of his office when he heard the door. Our eyes met, and I was thinking, 'Go back to your office.' He thought about it, you could see he did, but he came out.

"Broph went up to Frycer and said, 'Fuck you.' Frycer said, 'Fuck you.' That was their last conversation."

Since the Maple Leafs were the sporting focus of Toronto and Southern Ontario, there was no end of people connected with the team, mostly indirectly, who loved to pass along tips to the media. This involved everyone from staff at the nearby hotel where new players were housed to the janitors at the Gardens.

"There were leaks all over the place," Stellick said. "We knew there was a guy at Westbury Hotel who leaked stuff, and there was someone at Air Canada."

The latter leaker set off a comical scoop for radio station CFRB when the Air Canada source confused Tom McCarthy, who played for the Minnesota North Stars, with one of the Leafs' employees.

"We had a stick boy named Tom McCarthy," Stellick said. "One time we decided to take him on a road trip. Next thing you know, Bill Stephenson on CFRB breaks a story that the Leafs traded for Tom McCarthy. We denied there was a trade, but they stuck with the story.

"Finally, we figured out what happened, and when CFRB called again we told them, 'No, you got the stick boy.' The Air Canada guy saw his name on the manifest."

In Stellick's early years with the team, the Leafs flew commercial more than by charter, which led to a lot of shenanigans.

"Guys were competitive, and they were always betting on something," Stellick said. "They would put a buck each in the pot when we got off the plane, and the guy whose luggage came down the chute first would win. So they would all stand there and cheer the baggage, because they knew what some of them looked like.

"Once Stu Gavin's bag came off first and somebody hid it. He never knew his bag came off first, and they never found his bag."

On any flight, commercial or charter, players fell asleep at their peril.

"One time on a flight to Minnesota, Jim Korn fell asleep," Stellick said. "When he woke up, there was shaving cream on his head, a cigarette in his mouth, and he had no shoes.

"He never found his shoes and had to walk through the Minneapolis airport in January in his socks."

Practical jokes were not limited to team flights, of course. One of the better ones came during training camp in St. Catharines, Ontario. The players were subjected to the daily rigours of calisthenics by an instructor. One day, a few of them knew the instructor was not coming the next day and decided to hire a substitute.

"There were about four or five guys in the bar the night before," Stellick said. "It was a strip bar, and they paid one of the strippers to show up as guest PT instructor. They let a few of the other guys in on it.

"When she showed up and took her jacket off, they all moved closer. Her outfit was low-cut spandex, and she was a knockout. They told her to pick on Al Secord because he wasn't in on the joke.

"She was not a hockey fan and had no idea who Secord was. She said, 'Al, will you help me?' Then she did every exercise up close to him, so her cleavage was in his face. Al was beet red, and the guys were laughing like crazy."

Russ Courtnall was a talented 18-year-old forward from Victoria, British Columbia, when he was drafted in the first round by the Maple Leafs in 1983. He was thrilled to be drafted by the Leafs, because his late father, who committed suicide when Courtnall was 13 years old, always dreamed of his son playing for the Maple Leafs. But his first meeting with owner Harold Ballard did not go the way of most boyish dreams of making the NHL.

"In August, Russ Courtnall came to town with his mom, Kathy, for the contract signing," Stellick said. "Later, he always talked about how well they treated his mom, but there was quite a surprise for them on that first day.

"They were sitting in Harold's office. A week earlier, there had been a surprise birthday party for Harold for his 80th birthday. While they talking, the air conditioning was on, and from the back, this inflatable woman came flying along about three feet off the floor.

"It was one of those inflatable sex dolls, and someone had given it to Harold as a gag gift on his birthday. Russ and his mom saw it first, as they were chatting with Harold. Then Harold saw it and says, 'Oh, sorry about that, it was just a gift from my birthday,' and pushes it into another room like it was nothing unusual."

One part of Stellick's job, no matter his title at the time, was dealing with Ballard's girlfriend, Yolanda. She wormed her way into Ballard's life not long after serving a jail sentence for some funny business involving a will that was changed to benefit her and a lawyer friend. Her goal was to marry Ballard, which she never pulled off, although she legally changed her surname from McMillan to Ballard. She did, however, come to have great influence over Ballard as his health declined in the late 1980s.

"I got along really well with Yolanda because I knew what she was all about," Stellick said. "Harold always had a funny way of dealing with her. He would push her away at first, but he would always give in.

"I would talk to Gord Finn, who ran the box office, and he would lament she'd call on Monday for a Saturday game and order 12 tickets. So he'd check with Harold, and Harold would say, 'Tell her to go screw herself.'

"Then, as the week went on, Harold would say, 'Oh, those four are for her hairdresser? They're okay. Those four are for that person? They're okay.' I'd tell Gord, "Why are you getting caught up in this? You know how it's going to end up on Saturday, just set the tickets aside.'"

It was the same way when it came to the Leafs' travel plans. The only thing Ballard stayed firm on was that Yolanda was not allowed on the Leafs charter.

"He'd start off saying, 'Don't tell her where we going,'" Stellick said. "I remember we were in Chicago once and she showed up at the Stadium. I said, 'Yolanda's outside,' and he grinned, like he's happy she figured it out and showed up. She would always show up on her own.

"So Harold was shaving in the dressing room at Chicago Stadium. He went out in the hallway where she was and started giving her shit. 'What the hell are you doing here?' all that kind of thing. It would happen all the time.

"Finally, I said to Yolanda, 'Here's our travel book, here's our travel agent, you handle it.' That worked fine, and on every trip the call would come from his room, 'Oh, Nutsy Fagan is here today, get her a ticket.' Once she was there, he wanted to treat her right. I just said, 'Why do I want to get in this game?'"

Nutsy Fagan, by the way, was Ballard's favourite nickname for Yolanda. It came from the late Ted Reeve, an athlete and sportswriter for many years in Toronto who invented a long cast of sporting characters for his columns, Nutsy Fagan being one of them.

Ballard was one of Canada's most famous diabetics who never followed the diet guidelines for those with the disease. Yolanda made it her mission to see that Ballard ate properly, which caused more problems for the Leafs staff.

"She would order these ridiculous amounts of food for Harold in the hotels," Stellick said. "She always billed them to my room. I'd get a knock from room service, and there was a bill for three hundred bucks signed to my room.

"Then I'd get a call from Harold. He'd say, 'Christ, you can't believe the food they gave me.' He thought it was all free, that the hotel comped it."

By the early 1980s, the Leafs were flying charter flights almost all of the time. This made travel much easier, at least for a while. Ballard's legendary temper, though, ensured there were problems ahead.

"We chartered with Air Ontario, and we had one flight home that went terribly bad," Stellick said. "It started when the stewardess came by with a cheese tray and Harold went to grab it. She says, 'No, no, you can't have two kinds of cheese. I have to see if it lasts to the back.

"So he throws the first cheese back and is dropping f-bombs all over the place. Then we had to land in London [Ontario] because Toronto was fogged in. The flight crew was happy because they were based in London. But Harold was still fuming because the flight attendant pissed him off. He decreed we were not going charter anymore.

"I had to change all the flight arrangements. For the next six weeks, all I was doing were stupid commercial arrangements. But then Harold got in a fight on U.S. Air with one of the flight attendants. I remember

Guy Kinnear [the team trainer, who was tight with Ballard] had the itinerary for the next trip. U.S. Air was one of the flights, and Guy says, 'Gordie, wrong.'

"So we made our peace with Air Ontario after two months, and we were back on the charter."

Bob Stellick stayed much longer with the Maple Leafs than his older brother Gord, lasting until the fall of 1998 as the team's director of business operations and communications. He now runs his own company, Stellick Marketing Communications, Inc.

Along with Gord, Bob Stellick spent a lot of time in the company of Leafs owner Harold Ballard from the time he was hired by the Leafs through to Ballard's death in April 1990. Bob and Harold developed a close friendship, but there was a night when he thought it would come to an end. Luckily for him, Inge Hammarstrom, a former Leaf who once drew Ballard's public ire because he wanted no part of the fighting common in the NHL in the 1970s, came to his rescue.

"We were in Minnesota for a game, and Mr. Ballard was in a wheelchair," Bob Stellick said. "I was taking him down a ramp at the Met Center. We started picking up a bit of speed. There was a quarter-inch piece of plywood at the bottom, and I figured I could get the wheelchair over it with no problem.

"I hit it, and the wheelchair didn't go over it. It flipped forward and Mr. Ballard started flying out like Superman. Luckily, Inge Hammarstrom was standing there—he was at the game because he's a scout for the Philadelphia Flyers—and Inge ended up catching Mr. Ballard and putting him back in the wheelchair.

"How's that for irony? Inge Hammarstrom was ripped once by Mr. Ballard, and now he's working for the Philadelphia Flyers. Inge says, 'Bob, it looked like you tried to kill your boss.'

"He probably saved my job and saved Mr. Ballard from doing a face plant at the Met Center."

One of the people around Maple Leaf Gardens that Stellick recalls fondly was King Clancy. He had the longest tenure of anyone in the organization, but by the 1980s he was essentially paid to be Ballard's friend.

"King Clancy was a character," Stellick said. "We made the playoffs in 1986, and he would take the secretaries, Ellen and Mary, to Mass at St. Mike's every day to pray for the Leafs.

"But he was a terrible driver at that point. I think the guys at the Hot Stove Lounge used to fix it so he could keep his licence without taking the test. He'd be bouncing off the curbs, and the secretaries were more worried about their lives than the Leafs.

"We swept Chicago in that series, but we didn't know if it was more about him or the fact the secretaries prayed for their own salvation."

Ballard's other great friend was his dog, T.C. Puck. Various employees around the Gardens were stuck looking after the mutt at different times, and the dog's presence even came to annoy the players as they gathered on the Gardens ice surface for the annual team photograph.

"Our team photo was always a pain because Mr. Ballard insisted T.C. Puck had to be in it," Stellick said. "It wasn't a good picture unless it was a good picture of Puck. But we had a real problem year after year. Puck wouldn't sit still, so it didn't matter if it was a good picture of everyone or not, it had to be the one where Puck sat still.

"It wasn't until the fourth year [of having the dog] that Yolanda solved the problem. She figured out that Puck's balls were cold when he sat on the ice, so she put a towel underneath him and he sat quite happily. We all said, 'Gee, the poor guy, no wonder he didn't take a good picture. His balls were frozen.'"

This was not the only adventure the Gardens staff had with Ballard and animals, although the worst one was caused by his Yolanda and came in the wake of a gift from Ballard's friend Steve Stavro.

"Steve Stavro gave them a pair of geese for [Ballard's] cottage," Stellick said. "The geese had their wings clipped so they couldn't fly. When winter came, Yolanda figured they would freeze to death up at the cottage.

"She brought them down to the Gardens and put Pampers on them. They were running around [Ballard's] apartment. Yolanda didn't know what to do with them. But she couldn't keep the diapers on them. They were in there for a week, and we had to get them out of there."

Once Ballard took up residence at Maple Leaf Gardens in the apartment he had built, life changed for the staff.

"The secretaries ended up seeing him in his underwear or bathrobe when he came out to get his mail early in the morning," Stellick said. "That was always an interesting visual for anyone at 8:30 in the morning.

"His first line to me at that time of day was always, 'When are the world champions practicing?' He always called the Leafs that."

One of the problems with Ballard's ownership of the Maple Leafs was that he was preoccupied with all of the wrong things, including a Canadian Football League team he bought almost on a whim.

"He had a funny obsession with press clippings," Stellick said. "Pat Park, who is now the PR guy, was an intern then. Pat's main job was to get clippings for Mr. Ballard, who could never remember his name. He called him Murphy because he couldn't remember his name.

"Pat could be splitting the atom or designing a new breakout play, but if he didn't have Mr. Ballard's clips done, there would be hell to pay. They had to be slid under his door first thing in the morning.

"I learned early on that success was measured on different levels there. That was part of the problem—keeping Mr. Ballard happy took so much energy. Gord [Stellick] used to joke we were first class for all the wrong reasons. If someone's mother or wife got sick, we'd fly them to the Mayo Clinic. But we didn't spend any money on players.

"When Gord was GM, our payroll was under five million bucks. But we were losing almost that much on the Hamilton Tiger-Cats [of the CFL]. We were a 33-million-dollar-a-year company, and we were losing four million dollars a year on the Ticats. We could have bought Wayne Gretzky every year. So for Harold and King to go to the Ticat games, it cost about $400,000 a game, which was more than the entire gate [receipts] of the game."

Ballard was the first Leaf owner to regularly rent out Maple Leaf Gardens to other acts, something he started when he took control of the business side of the operation when Conn Smythe was still the majority owner. Stellick said Ballard had an interest in most of the other shows but was especially keen on one, perhaps because the old huckster felt a kinship with them.

"He was always fascinated with televangelists," Stellick said. "They had Jimmy Swaggert at the building once, and there were green garbage cans all over where people would throw everything they owned into them, including their watches and rings. Mr. Ballard always admired guys who could get people to do that."

But Ballard's admiration had a limit.

"Then he found out Jimmy Swaggert was selling Bibles and Mr. Ballard wasn't getting a cut," Stellick said. "So he got mad and was fighting for a deal to get his percentage. When that didn't work out,

he had his car parked on the on-ramp so Jimmy Swaggert couldn't get his limo into the building. He had to walk in like the rest of the people."

Ballard was even an innovator at times, although this was more accidental than not.

"Mr. Ballard did a lot of things to get reaction," Stellick said. "He knew the difference between page 88 and page one. He kept the media at bay until he wanted them and then, bang bang, off he'd go.

"Once, when the Hamilton Tiger-Cats played the Toronto Argos in the playoffs, there were no rink board ads in the building, so Mr. Ballard put Ticat rink boards up. They were the first rink-board ads in the NHL and they were Ticat logos.

"He got fined by the NHL. Then he put the logos in the ice and said, 'I don't care.'"

Ballard's love for both attention and his Tiger-Cats football team lead him to do some risky things in a name of promotion. He loved to wave the Tiger-Cats banner at Toronto hockey fans, who responded angrily because most of them were Toronto Argonaut fans.

"One time he decided to do a big PR stunt with a tiger," Stellick said. "Somehow, he came up with a tiger, and the first idea was Mr. Ballard was to go on the ice and walk the tiger around the ice while everyone boos him. The tiger was to be drugged so he wouldn't do anything dangerous.

"But they didn't give the tiger enough drugs. He was not quite doped up enough. They were trying to get him into a convertible because then the idea was that Harold would drive around with the tiger in the passenger seat. But they couldn't get the tiger in the car.

Harold Ballard defined the term eccentric owner.

"Mr. Ballard said, 'Well I got the tiger here, I want to do something.' He had the handler bring it out, and everyone was booing the tiger. Mr. Ballard ended up putting the tiger in a headlock. The tiger was not very happy. We were all going nuts because we thought Mr. Ballard was going to be eaten on the ice at Maple Leaf Gardens. But he survived."

Maple Leaf Gardens had a long history with animal acts, because one of the annual shows during Ballard's regime was the Garden Brothers Circus. This story began a little before the arrival of the circus when Bob Stellick's brother Gord landed his own parking spot, a perk that reflected his rising status at the Gardens.

"It was always funny when the circus came to the Gardens," Bob Stellick said. "I remember my brother Gord thinking he was finally a big wheel because he was a young guy and given his own parking spot. He was 22 years old.

"One day he was out there cleaning his car in his parking spot. Two drunks came out of the Hot Stove Lounge, and they were reading the names on the spots. They said, 'King Clancy, oh yeah, Punch Imlach, oh yeah. G. Stellick? Who the hell is G. Stellick?'

"Gordie said, very quietly, 'That's me.'

"His parking spot was right by the door, and later that spring, when the circus came, they used it to store the elephant shit. Gord pulled up to park and all the elephant shit was piled there. There was no room to park his car. So he knew he really hadn't made it yet."

The circus animals and the maintenance staff at the arena did not always get along, according to Bob Stellick.

"The Garden Brothers always had these crazy acts, and a lot involved chimpanzees," Stellick said. "The chimps were always dressed up like whatever was popular at the time. One year, they were Teenage Mutant Ninja Chimps. But people didn't realize chimps are scary and powerful.

"One of the maintenance guys would tease them every time they came off the stage. He would scratch his armpits and go, 'Ooohhh, ohh,' imitating the monkey.

"After four days, the last chimp off the stage had enough. He took off after the maintenance guy and chased him down the hall. The last I saw was this guy running down the hall, about to get killed by a chimp with a breast plate looking like a Teenage Mutant Chimp."

Even Ballard could not escape the wrath of the circus animals.

"They had lions, who were kept chained up in cages back by the Zamboni with the elephants," Stellick said. "One year, Mr. Ballard kept bugging one of the lions all week. He would poke it through bars with his cane.

"Finally, at the end of the week, the lion peed on him."

By the mid-1980s, the Leafs were falling behind on the NHL's move to sign European players. After seeing a few too many other teams spirit players out from behind the Iron Curtain, the Leafs decided to get in on the bonanza. General manager Gerry McNamara landed several players from Czechoslovakia in the next few years. The best was Peter Ihnacak, a hard-nosed but low-scoring centre who played for the Leafs for eight years. The worst was Miroslav Ihnacak, Peter's younger brother.

McNamara said the younger Ihnacak was a big, strong forward who was going to be a star in the NHL. Ballard was convinced to shell out $100,000 to get him out of Czechoslovakia, which included bribes for the right people. But the Stellick brothers and the rest of Leaf management came in for a shock when Miro Ihnacak arrived at the airport in Toronto.

"This was a big clandestine thing. Mr. Ballard paid a big bribe to get Miro out," Bob Stellick said. "I was getting the press release done, and I described Miro Ihnacak as 6-foot-1, 195 pounds.

"Then Gord called from the airport, and I asked him how it was going. Gord said, 'We got him here.' I said, 'How is he?' Gord asked if I was working on the press release. I said, 'Yeah.' Then Gord said, 'I don't know, maybe it's just me, but the weight of Communism seems to have worn Miro down. I think he's about 5-9. He's my size.'

"So I had to change the press release. It went downhill from there."

Miro Ihnacak was a Leaf for 55 games over the 1985-86 and 1986-87 seasons. Given the buildup before he arrived, Miro was awarded No. 27, which had been worn by Leaf greats Frank Mahovlich and Darryl Sittler. He was also handed a multiyear contract for a total of $650,000. For all that money, the Leafs received eight goals and nine assists in those 55 games.

But that contract was not quite that rich when Miro arrived, which led to a nasty scene in the Leafs dressing room.

"We thought we had signed Miro, and then Peter decided his brother didn't sign for enough money," Bob Stellick said. "He said, 'Why play for soup money?' Dan Maloney was the coach, and he got mad. He ordered [trainer] Guy Kinnear to get Miro's equipment in the dressing room.

"People were around, the media and everything, and Dan threw Miro's equipment out in the hallway. Two days before, this guy was our new superstar, a 6-1, 195-pound glory boy, and now he was 5-9, 160 pounds, and his equipment was getting thrown out the door."

Even by the standards of NHL owners, Ballard was not especially enlightened. When his fellow owners grudgingly came to accept the presence of women reporters in their dressing rooms in the 1970s, Ballard held out. He refused to allow them into the Leafs dressing room, and rather than comply with the NHL's order for equal access, Ballard closed the room to all reporters. Interviews were done in the hall to the discomfort of all concerned.

Things came to a head on February 4, 1987, when the Toronto media got together and decided to force their way into the Leafs dressing room en masse after the game. That was the closest Bob Stellick remembers ever coming to losing his job.

"My lowest point was the Charge of the Light Brigade night," he said. "Harold Ballard didn't want women in dressing room. The NHL said if you won't let women in, you have to close off the room, so we closed it.

"Then everyone piled through one night. Mr. Ballard came in and started yelling at [Gunner] Kinnear. Gunner said, 'It's Stellick's fault. It's Stellick's job to keep them out.' And it was my job. I was as white as a ghost. Then Ballard got into it with Bill Houston [of *The Globe and Mail*]."

The next morning, all of the Toronto newspapers were full of pictures and stories about the charge into the dressing room. Ballard remained angry about it for a while, but Stellick kept his job. And women were eventually allowed into the Leafs dressing room.

The players kept Stellick on his toes as well, especially on the road. He never knew what to expect when the phone rang in his hotel room. The western trips in the 1980s were particularly prone to mischief.

"In those days, L.A. was the only place to get warm during the season," Stellick said. "Next door to our hotel was a Carl's Jr. burger. One night, Jeff Reese and Bob Halkidis, who used to play for the Los Angeles Kings, were out riding around with a buddy of Halkidis's from L.A.

"They decided to go to the Carl's drive-through before they went back to the hotel. When they were in the drive-through, someone put a gun to their heads and they got robbed. That was typical of an L.A. trip, it seemed at the time."

The players never tired of practical jokes, either on themselves or on each other, most of which were pulled on the airplane or at the airport.

"Doug Gilmour was always a funny guy," Stellick said. "He would do the pranks if you were killing time at the airport because you had to fly commercial. He would take a thread from the sewing kit in his hotel room and tie a $20 bill to it. Then he would put it on the floor and pull it back when people would try to pick it up. It was amazing how many people would get mad.

"The worst prank anyone played on a player was on Don Edwards. This was toward the end of his career [as a goaltender], and he had had a few run-ins with some of the guys.

"We flew home at two in the morning one time. Before we left on the trip, some of the guys loosened the lug nuts on his Corvette in the underground parking garage at the airport. He had a really nice Corvette. Edwards came wheeling out in the thing, and one of his wheels went bouncing down the ramp. The other one popped out and ripped the fibreglass fender on the Corvette.

"For a long time, we all thought someone had tried to steal his tires because there was a big issue back then about people driving around the airport stealing wheels. But I heard years later it was a teammate who did it. That was a cruel prank."

One of the players who gave Leafs management the most trouble was enforcer John Kordic. He had a number of off-ice issues and died at the age of 27 in 1992 during a confrontation with police that was fuelled by a cocaine and steroid binge.

Discipline problems with the ill-tempered Kordic were common. After one blow-up, Kordic was sent down to the Leafs' farm team in Newmarket, a bedroom community just north of Toronto.

"When he got sent down, we had an intern in Newmarket named Al Miller," Stellick said. "He is now the general manager of a major-junior team, but then he was a 19-year-old intern for us.

"Kordic didn't show up in Newmarket, and a radio station called the team. Al Miller answered the phone. When the radio guy said Kordic didn't show up, Al said, 'He better show up if he wants to get a pay cheque.' The station ran that clip all day.

John Kordic's days with the Leafs were rarely happy.

"Kordic got pretty upset, so we told Al Miller that Kordic was going to beat the crap out of him. He spent a week hiding from Kordic."

Kordic's last season with the Leafs was 1990-91, and his demotion to the Newmarket Saints of the American Hockey League came just before he was traded to the Washington Capitals. His stay in Newmarket lasted just eight games, which did not surprise Stellick.

"By the second team meeting, Kordic fell asleep in the middle of it and started snoring," Stellick said. "So you knew things would not go well for him up there. That was the end of the Kordic era in Toronto."

For years, the Leafs tried to help Kordic deal with his addictions. But he either rejected the attempts out of hand or accepted them grudgingly and made only half-hearted attempts to get better.

"Through Jim McKenny, we got him in a rehab centre once," Stellick said. "The centre partnered its patients with people, and Kordic was given a partner. Kordic asked his partner about his nationality, and when he said Greek, Kordic said, 'At the Gardens, the Greek guys clean the toilets.'

"That was the end of him helping Kordic. In fact, that was the last gasp of anyone trying to help him."

As director of public relations, Stellick was expected by Harold Ballard to control what appeared in the media about the Leafs. Naturally, this was an impossible task. When your team was the focus of every media outlet in town, some days were more impossible than others.

"When the guys were all young, the Star took a picture of Steve Thomas, Gary Leeman, Russ Courtnall, Wendel Clark, and Al Iafrate, all with their shirts off in the dressing room," Stellick said. "It was a *Young Guns*–type picture, and they ran it big.

"Then later on there was a raid on a bathhouse in Toronto, and the picture was plastered all over the walls. Next thing you know, rumours were all over town that the Leafs were involved in bathhouses."

Bob Stellick added the title of manager of business operations to his portfolio after Cliff Fletcher became president and GM of the Maple Leafs in 1991. He was responsible for handling the team's charter flights. For years, the Leafs flew on a Convair 580, a turbo-prop plane. It was an old plane, but it was handy in one respect, which was why the Leafs kept using it.

"The noise rules allowed only turbo-prop planes to fly into Toronto after midnight," Stellick said. "A turbo-prop could fly in until four in the morning, so it was the better plane to use."

The powers that be, however, decided the Convair was too long in the tooth for the Leafs, and Stellick was ordered to find a new plane.

"We got a Dash 8, which I think was a new turbo-prop," he said. "So for a preseason game in Montreal we rented this Dash 8 from somebody at the [Toronto] Island Airport. But the plane was too small for us, and it was slower than the Convair."

This did not go over well with the players and especially with the head coach, Pat Burns, a man who was easily stirred to anger.

"Pat Burns was really cheesed off," Stellick said. "He kept saying, 'I could walk faster than this thing flies.' Then, six months later, the guy I leased the plane from got arrested for selling parts to Iraq. He was using his company to ship aviation parts to enemies of the United States.

"Thank God I only rented it from him once, so I wasn't in the middle of a treason charge."

Mike Murphy succeeded Burns as head coach for the 1996-97 season, and he also had some aircraft demands. But he came to regret them when the team flew home after a game.

"We had a trip to St. Louis, and Mike Murphy wanted a faster plane," Stellick said. "We had a home-and-home series against the Blues. Every year, the transport authority would give us a few exemptions to fly in late on a jet. So we spent all this extra money to charter an Air Canada jet for the trip, and it ended up being 40 minutes faster.

"But it turned out a whole bunch of guys got off the plane and went to a strip joint near the airport. Someone phoned The Fan [a radio station] the next day and said, 'I saw the Leafs lose last night, and then I saw a bunch of them at The Landing Strip.' It turned out we paid four times as much as our regular charter so the guys could have more beer at the strip joint."

The beginning of the end of Stellick's tenure with the Leafs came when Steve Stavro used his leverage as co-executor of Harold Ballard's estate to grab control of the franchise. Stavro made his fortune through the

Knob Hill Farms chain of grocery stores.

Donald Giffin, one of the other executors, succeeded Ballard as president of Maple Leaf Gardens, but he was soon swept away by Stavro in the nasty fight for the company. One thing Giffin accomplished was to install Cliff Fletcher as president and GM over Stavro's objections.

"Mr. Stavro didn't trust any of us because we were all Cliff guys, and he wanted to get rid of Cliff," Stellick said. "I remember the first meeting we had [after Stavro took over]. We were talking about how people were compensated.

"[Stavro] said, 'Well, at Knob Hill Farms we give Old World bonuses.' Everybody started wondering if at the end of the day you had a live sheep stuck in your trunk. It was a very, very strange time that way."

Bob Stellick found himself a target of the wrath of Stavro and the other Gardens directors over a trophy. The J.P. Bickell Memorial trophy used to be awarded to someone whom the directors felt made a superior contribution to the franchise that season. It was introduced by Conn Smythe and was not awarded if the directors felt there was no suitable candidate. During Ballard's ownership, the trophy was pushed aside, like many other Gardens traditions. When Stavro came in, he wanted to revive the award, but by then the trophy had been put to another use.

"We re-christened it," Stellick said. "It was sitting in a vault at the Gardens, this old vault, and we re-christened it the King Clancy Cup for the annual Montreal–Toronto alumni game.

"We had a beautiful marble base made for it. It was gorgeous, and we put it on display in the lobby. I would take it down to Montreal on the train in a gym bag for the game.

"Then Mr. Stavro took over, and the directors wanted to revive the Bickell Trophy because it was awarded by them. So there was this indignation that what I had done was horrible. Mr. Stavro was angry.

"Actually, the only thing I was remiss on was when they took the Bickell back to have my bottom taken off. It was reappraised, and it turned out to be worth something like one hundred and ten thousand dollars because it was solid gold.

"I kept thinking about how I was sticking it on trains. I didn't think it was worth that much so it was no big deal then."

After Stavro took over the Leafs, there were many changes, including the addition of a mascot, Carlton the Bear, and therein lies a tale. The idea for a mascot came up when Stellick and his fellow marketers found it increasingly difficult to get the highly paid players to make personal appearances on behalf of the team.

Stellick and the Leafs media relations director, Pat Park, held a meeting with the marketing and community relations departments to discuss the mascot. Christie Fletcher, the daughter of Cliff, the GM and president, was also at the meeting. She proved to be an enthusiastic albeit naïve, young employee.

"We had this idea of a bear done up, and now we were wondering what to call him," Stellick said. "Pat said, 'Why don't we name him Carlton after the street we're on?' Everyone said that was a great idea. Then we started wondering what number the bear should wear.

"Christie Fletcher said, 'Why not use number 69?' We had people from the [mascot] manufacturer there too, and all these people went dead silent and looked at Christie. Finally someone says, 'What do you mean?'

"Christie says, 'Well, 69 is the address for Maple Leaf Gardens.' I said, 'Well, Christie, the address is actually 60 Carlton, but we like the way you're thinking.'"

Carlton got number 60.

There were fewer public-relations crises without Ballard around, but the Stavro regime still managed to cause a lot of self-inflicted damage. The worst was the sex abuse scandal, when it was discovered a few employees used the lure of Maple Leaf Gardens to sexually abuse children for years, sometimes on the premises.

Stellick was pushed aside by Stavro and his lawyer, Brian Bellmore, after the news broke. They brought in an outside public relations company for spin control, and it was a disaster. The lowest point came when Stellick was forced to stand helplessly at the back of the room while Bellmore clumsily conducted a press conference and came across as unsympathetic to the victims. One of the victims later committed suicide.

Stellick bit his tongue, however, and remained loyal to his employers. Ken Dryden, a Toronto native who was a Hall of Fame goaltender for the Montreal Canadiens in the 1970s, replaced Fletcher as president and GM of the Leafs in 1997. That was when Stellick knew it was time to leave.

"I realized it right from the very beginning," Stellick said. "Ken showed me his opening speech, and it had the words Stanley Cup in it 23 times."

Stellick knew this was a sensitive term in a city that had not won the Stanley Cup since 1967. There was a lot of potential for ridicule from the media and anger from the fans.

"So I went back to him and said, 'Ken, no ownership throws around the words Stanley Cup lightly. Maybe you could use the word winning and use it lightly.' Ken was very thoughtful, but he came back and said he was going to stick with Stanley Cup.

"I thought okay, but it's not that easy to win, Ken. This is not Montreal. Look around, you don't have the roster. His opening speech was all about imagining a 15-goal scorer becoming a 30-goal scorer.

"I can imagine that all I want, but it's not going to happen. That was the end for me. Ken was a nice guy, but I thought it was time to move on."

5

BONESY AND WILBUR

Joe Bowen became the play-by-play voice of the Toronto Maple Leafs at the start of the 1982-83 season and has been going strong ever since. The emphasis is on *strong*, as the native of Sault Ste. Marie, Ontario, has a voice that does not need any amplification. He has gone through several sidekicks over the years on Maple Leafs radio and television broadcasts, from Gary Monahan to Bill Watters to Jim Ralph to Harry Neale.

Watters joined the Leafs radio team in 1985 while he was still a player agent. Wilbur and Bonesy, as they called each other, hit it off immediately and formed a close friendship. But there was one night early in the relationship when Bowen thought he was going to lose his sidekick.

The scene was up in the rafters of the old Chicago Stadium, where one of the attendants in the radio booth kept a supply of strong drink.

"The guy had this old file cabinet, one that Al Capone probably used, and he kept a bottle of rye in it," Bowen said. "Halfway through the second period, he would ask Wilbur if he wanted an out-of-town scoreboard. Then he would pour a mittful of whiskey in this glass and add a little bit of Coke or whatever Wilbur was drinking. He'd have about three or four of these out-of-town scoreboards.

"We used to joke about it on the air. I'd say, 'Here's Wilbur with another out-of-town scoreboard.' We finished the game, and we were walking along the upper balcony. There was not an elevator or escalator in the joint. The poor concession guys had to lug everything up 94 stairs—I counted—hot dogs, pop, beer kegs, everything.

"We're walking along this thing, and some guy had dropped a Mason jar of relish on the top step, right where we went down. Now in Wilbur's myopic condition, he couldn't see it. He hit the relish, and it was like a luge competition. He went down about ten stairs, just boom, boom, boom.

"He got up, he had relish in his hair, on his coat, his coat was ripped, there was relish everywhere. He'd had about five out-of-town scoreboards before he hit the top stair. I yelled, 'Wilbur if you'd just bounced off the wall, you'd have been like the luge at the Olympics and gone 94 stairs to the basement. But he was all right."

Bowen's first job as a broadcaster for a professional team was with the Halifax Voyageurs, the Montreal Canadiens' old farm team in the American Hockey League. The coach of the Voyageurs for one of those seasons was John Brophy. They developed a friendship that continued after Brophy joined the Toronto Maple Leafs.

"After each game with the Voyageurs, I went out with Broph," Bowen said. "I loved Broph dearly. We'd get out, and he'd be saying, 'I can't stand this guy, that guy can't do this.' Once in a while, he would say something I'd disagree with, and we would get into a full-fledged argument. Sometimes it would get to real fuck-you fights. The next day, everything would be fine.

"One time with the Leafs, we went to a game in Minnesota and for the first time we stayed downtown [in Minneapolis]. They had an Italian restaurant in the hotel where the waiters and waitresses sang arias. It was like a little dinner theatre.

"Bob Stellick took all of us out for dinner—the writers, broadcasters, and coaches. We were having a nice meal on the Leafs. This didn't happen every day with Harold Ballard's chequebook.

"After copious amounts of wine and a couple of arias, Broph piped up and said, 'I'm going to send Chris McRae out tomorrow night to fight his brother [Basil, who played for the North Stars].' I said, 'Broph, fuck off. I've got three sons, and one of my boys will never go out and fight his brother because the coach says so.'

"Brophy said, '[Chris McRae] will take his pants down at the corner of Yonge and Eglinton if I say so and if he wants to stay on this team. He'll fight his brother.' We had a real big argument. The people at the other tables were looking. I said, 'Broph, if you think that, then the game has passed you by.' Well, he went off like Mount St. Helen's. He was screaming, 'I don't have to listen to this shit, fuck you,' and he stormed out.

"All the other guys were going, 'Geez, this is it. You've done it now.' But at seven o'clock the next morning, the phone rang. It was Broph. He said, 'What are you doing?'

"'Nothing.'

"'Coming for breakfast?'

"'Yeah, all right.'

"And that was Broph. He would just go completely off on you and then forget about it. That was the night's entertainment; he didn't care."

One Leaf coach who had a little harder time letting go after an argument was Dan Maloney. Bowen says he still feels guilty for his part in a bad night for Maloney. This also happened in Minnesota, and it came just after GM Gerry McNamara and Brophy took the captain's C away from Rick Vaive for sleeping in and missing practice.

"Tom Reid, who played for Minny but now did radio, asked us out for beverages after the game," Bowen said. "I saw [assistant coach] Claire Alexander and Danny Maloney and said, 'Tom wants to take us out.' They said, 'Sure, after the weekend we just had, sure.' It was a good session, but we got back to the hotel and found out World War III had broken out.

"The house dick at the Marriott was there. Somebody, one of the players, had ripped the phone off the wall of one of the elevators. All of the players had gone out because we were flying back to Toronto the next morning. After having to deal with Rick Vaive and losing the game, Maloney was in no humour to handle this. He went nuts in the hallway.

"Claire Alexander went into [defenceman] Bill Root's room and found him hiding under the bed. Rooter said, 'You've got to get out there. He's going to kill somebody.'

"'Claire said, 'Not me. I'm not going out there, he'll kill me.'

"When it was just starting to quiet down, the elevator door opened and out came another player with a little damsel on his arm. I don't know why I was still there. Boom! The Irish temper kicked in. Maloney had the player up against the wall, and his fist was cocked. He was going to put the guy right through the drywall. Brad Smith was hanging on to his arm, trying to hold him back, and he did. Thank God Smitty did, because Maloney would have plowed the guy something terrible.

"The next day, it was really quiet on the way home. I always thought I shouldn't have brought Danny with us that night. It wasn't the right thing to do at the time."

Like just about everyone else connected with the Leafs, Bowen found himself a target of Ballard's ire. The difference was that at least once, thanks to the fact his employer was radio rights holder Telemedia, and not Ballard, Bowen was able to take his revenge.

"Harold wouldn't let [the radio crew] fly on the Leafs charter," Bowen said. "We always flew American Airlines. If you were a frequent flyer with them, you used to be able to buy stickers to upgrade to first class if you had a full-fare [economy] ticket, which we always had. You could take that sticker to the check-in desk, and if there was room in first class, you could upgrade for 15 dollars. Wilbur and I used to do that all the time.

"So we're out in Los Angeles, and the Leafs are flying home on American Airlines because it's too far for their charter plane. Gordie Stellick is running around in a panic because he can't get Harold bumped up to first class. There was no room.

"Gordie tells me I have to give him my ticket. I said, 'No way, I'm keeping this one.' As soon as they made the first-class announcement, I bolted for the door, got my beverage going from the stewardess, got the newspaper. Harold gets on, and I said, 'Harold, good to see you. How are you? Gee, this is a tough road trip.' He grumped and groaned, and said, 'What are you doing up here?'

"Gord was behind him, and he was in a complete state. I did it because three weeks earlier in Chicago, it was snowing like hell. You remember how tough it was to get a cab out of that old stadium? Well, the Leaf bus pulled out and Harold gave me the big wave as they went by. I had to wait forever to get a cab because nobody liked to come out there, the neighbourhood was so bad.

"So when I got on that plane in L.A., I sat there in that first-class seat and gave Harold the old wave as he went by, too."

Flying from Toronto to Hartford in the years before the Hartford Whalers became the Carolina Hurricanes was always an adventure. The big airline companies only offered a few flights to Hartford, so trips were often made with small, little-known airlines.

Bowen and Jim O'Leary, who covered the Leafs for the *Toronto Sun* at the time, once found themselves the only passengers on a small plane operated by a company called Mall Airlines. For a while, they both thought this would be the last flight of their lives.

"Jim and I got on this two-engine prop job to get to Hartford," Bowen said. "It was a gorgeous, sunny day, and I stopped at the duty-free store and bought nice big bottle of Baileys. Jim and I were the only passengers. The plane was so small—there were three seats on each side of the aisle plus the pilot and co-pilot.

"After we're in the air for a while, I looked out the window and smoke was pouring out of the engine on my side. The pilot was about an arm's length away, so I said, 'Ah, buddy, we seem to have a little problem back here.' Then I heard these reassuring words from the cockpit: 'Holy shit!'

"The pilot shut down the engine and put a fire extinguisher on it and got it under control. We were flying with the one propeller. Both O'Leary and I figured this could be it.

"So what does the pilot do? O'Leary and I were right behind him, but he picked up the intercom. 'Ladies and gentlemen, we are flying on one engine, but do not be concerned. We are more than capable of flying with one engine. We will be touching down in Albany. However, I would take all sharp objects out of your pockets and really fasten your seatbelts.' Cripes, the guy was from me to you away and he was talking away on the intercom.

"I took out the bottle of Bailey's and said, 'If we're going down, we're not losing this.' Jim and I passed it back and forth, and it was gone real quick.

"The pilot put the plane down fine, though. As we were getting off the plane, we took our first good look at the pilots. Man, were they young. They looked like our paper boys. It must have been their first flight.

"I said to the guy, 'This ever happen before?' He could barely speak. He said, 'Ohhh, uhhhh,' and finally, 'Only on the simulator.'

"We got a flight on another airline for the rest of the trip to Hartford."

Since Ballard would not allow his girlfriend, Yolanda, to travel on the Leafs charter, Bowen and Watters often became her travelling companions on commercial flights. This was not always fun, given Yolanda's shopping habits and her tendency to misjudge how much luggage she had.

"She almost always was on our flight," Bowen said. "She was always nice to us. So once Wilbur offered her a ride to the airport in our cab. He told her all we had was our carry-on luggage, and Yolanda said that's all she had too.

"The next morning, after her shopping spree, which all got charged to Harold's room, seven strong men couldn't carry all the luggage she had. So there we were, struggling to carry all of the luggage, and she said, 'Sorry, boys, I must have needed just a few extra things.'"

On another occasion, Yolanda's loosey-goosey approach to travel forced Bowen to once again go beyond the call of duty.

"One night we were flying to Quebec, and Yolanda was on the plane," Bowen said. "We flew to Montreal and changed planes for Quebec. But Yolanda had only checked her luggage to Montreal. She says, 'What am I going to do?'

"We were standing at the baggage carrousel where it goes down into the luggage area. She said it's a blue bag, and I hopped on the conveyor belt and went down into the luggage area. The luggage handlers were all looking at me, and I said, 'Here's the problem, guys.' So we were holding up bags, and Yolanda was looking down from the little door. We were holding up bags, saying, 'Is this the one? No? How about this one?' Finally I got the right one, and I had to climb back up the belt out the little door to the baggage carrousel.

"Obviously, that was before 9/11."

As his health problems mounted, Ballard became less concerned with appearances and more concerned with comfort. This often came to the discomfort of those around him, especially when it came to the combination of his kidney problems and his arthritis.

"In Minnesota, the press box sloped up on both sides to centre ice, where the middle part was flat," Bowen said. "Our radio position was almost at the Leafs blue line, so we were on the incline. Harold sat almost at centre ice, right at the top of the incline. By that time, he had to pee a lot because of his kidneys, but his arthritis was so bad he couldn't get around, so he would often let it go wherever he happened to be.

"One night I look up and there is this stream of water coming down by my feet. I thought Wilbur spilled his pop. But Harold was having a pee, and it was flowing down by our feet. We had to lift our feet and do the broadcast in that position."

Bill Watters was a football player out of Orillia, Ontario, and later a teacher who always had a hankering to work in the hockey business. He scratched that itch in the 1970s when he went to work for notorious player agent Alan Eagleson before teaming up with Rick Curran to start Branada Sports, which represented many NHL players over the years.

His first love in hockey, though, was the Toronto Maple Leafs. He started working as a colour analyst on the Leafs radio broadcasts in the 1985-86 season, when he was still a player agent. There were lots of howls about the obvious conflict of interest because Watters had nine clients on the team.

But Watters was outspoken enough that Harold Ballard, the bombastic Leafs owner, twice tried to have him fired. Each time, Watters' employer, Telemedia Broadcasting Systems, managed to convince Ballard to back down.

In October 1991, Watters made the jump from the radio booth to the Leafs front office when general manager Cliff Fletcher hired him to be assistant GM. Watters spent 12 years in that job. He was pushed out in 2003 when John Ferguson, Jr., was hired as GM after Pat Quinn was forced to give up his GM portfolio and stick to coaching.

Watters is now back on radio on AM 640 in Toronto, and he is also a television commentator on Rogers Sportsnet. Looking back at how he first got into radio, Watters said it was a happy accident in September 1985.

"I had a private box, which I purchased from Maple Leaf Gardens," he said. "I used it for my clients when I was an agent. There was an exhibition game, and no one was using the box, so I took my family down.

"We were watching the game and Vicki McKee, who worked for Telemedia at the time, came into the box. I asked her what she was doing, and she told me she was auditioning prospects for the colour job."

Watters asked who the next person to audition was, and McKee mentioned a former NHL coach. Watters told her he could do a much better job than that fellow.

"So Vicki said, 'If you're such a big shot, why don't you try?' I said, 'Sure, when?' She told me I could do the third period. So I did.

"The next morning, I got a call from Gordie Stellick asking if I wanted to do it. I said sure. I also had nine clients on the team, so I defended myself for about six months. Those were some of the best years of my life."

But it was not the best paying job Watters had ever had. He soon found out that broadcasting was a labour of love. In those days, thanks to the effects of Harold Ballard's ownership on the fortunes of the Leafs, Telemedia was not making a great deal of money on the radio broadcasts. To keep expenses down, the company decreed the colour analyst would not do road games. Any available body in the other NHL city was hired to work with play-by-play man Joe Bowen.

With Watters on board, this changed. As a player agent, he could schedule meetings with clients in most of the cities the Leafs visited. But Watters was still paying his own way except for the meal money, and he was fortunate he and Bowen quickly became good friends.

"When we figured out how much they were paying us, we said we'd better room together," Watters said. "So we did and then tried to live on the per diem."

Although Watters took his share of shots from sportswriters and others questioning his obvious conflict of interest, the greatest threat to his job came from Harold Ballard. The Leafs owner did not like some of Watters' comments that were critical of the Leafs and tried on two occa-

sions to have him fired.

On the first occasion, Telemedia told Ballard that Watters was not going anywhere, and the owner backed off. But in September 1988, Ballard tried again. Watters thinks Ballard was egged on by his pal, the late Dick Beddoes. By then, Beddoes was no longer a newspaper columnist and worked for a television station in Hamilton with, Watters believes, designs on the job as Joe Bowen's sidekick.

Ballard wrote a letter to Telemedia demanding that Watters be replaced. This time he did not go away, so the two parties reached a compromise.

"Thank God Telemedia stood up for me, because I enjoyed doing it even though I wasn't making a fortune at it," Watters said. "Finally they said, 'Here's what we do, we'll put Dick on a pregame show.' That's what it was all about."

But it wasn't long before Watters incurred Ballard's wrath again.

"The Leafs had acquired Tom Kurvers for Scott Niedermayer," Watters said, referring to the infamous Floyd Smith trade in which he gave up the first-round pick that eventually became Niedermayer to the New Jersey Devils for a journeyman defenceman. "I said, 'If Kurvers is a top-six defenceman, my aunt's my uncle. He can't play.' Then I looked and saw Kenny Daniels, who was doing the radio play-by-play for Joe, shaking like a leaf."

Daniels, who filled in for Bowen when the latter was doing television games, had good reason to be frightened. This was around the time Dave Hodge was fired as host of the Leafs' mid-week television games on the Global television network. Hodge was dumped for being critical of the Leafs, and many suspected Ballard's fingerprints were on the move even though his health was declining rapidly at the time. A more likely culprit was Smith, the Leafs GM who was taking shots for his trades from all sides.

"The next day, after they let Hodge go, I got a call from Bob Stellick, who was a good friend," Watters said. "He said, 'Willie, don't say that

---

Bill Watters went from broadcaster to Leaf executive and back to broadcaster.

again or you'll be gone next.' So I had to cut back on my bombastic style. That's when Smitty was running the show."

Before Smith went after him, Watters had to withstand a couple attempts on his coaching job by John Brophy. They were headed for trouble because many of Watters' clients—Rick Vaive, Al Iafrate and Gary Leeman—were not Brophy's favourite players. Despite this, Watters and Brophy got along well enough for long stretches.

"Once, we got going about Ricky [Vaive] because Ricky was a client and I still had the conflict," Watters said. "That happened in St. Louis with [assistant coach Garry] Lariviere and Brophy. Then we really got into it again in Pittsburgh.

"I don't think he ever took me seriously, because I'd say to him, 'Broph, you better hit me hard with your first shot because you won't get another one.' It was something you'd say and hope he wouldn't, because I'm a lover not a fighter. I was the gambler on that one. I was playing my ace card. He just laughed, and that was it."

Watters can remember a few laughs with Ballard, especially during his days as an agent before he took up radio work.

"I had a tough negotiation with the Leafs over Gary Leeman," Watters said. "Now it was time to get the first cheque, which was the first portion of the signing bonus. The cheque came to our office, and it was for something around fifty thousand bucks.

"Harold had wonderful penmanship, and he wrote out the cheque and signed it himself. Right where it says *item* on the cheque, Harold wrote, 'Bill, you're a crook.'"

A few years later, Watters saw how tough Harold could be.

"One of stories about Harold I remember best was at a morning skate when we were in the Hot Stove Lounge talking to him," Watters said. "Yolanda came around the corner and said, 'Harold, did you take your medication?' Harold said no, and Yolanda went to get the insulin shot.

"Harold was wearing a pair of corduroy pants, and Yolanda brought in the insulin needle. She whipped it out and jabbed it into his leg right through the pants. Harold said, 'There, now get out of here.'

"What a tough old prick. He was a beauty."

Later, after he went to work for the Leafs as the assistant GM to Cliff Fletcher, Watters found himself dealing with another tough customer, head coach Pat Burns.

Like many NHL coaches, Burns was a fellow who had more faith in his veteran players. He didn't hate rookies, he just liked his chances of winning—and keeping his job—better with the guys who had been around the block.

The boss, Fletcher, also had a reputation for preferring veteran players. But less so than Burns, since Fletcher was a GM and it was his job to develop young players for the team. Watters remembers this as a minor source of friction between the two. Through Watters, Fletcher would often ask Burns to play the youngsters more.

"And Burnsie would always tell me," Watters recalls with a laugh. "Wilbur, if Cliff wants me to play the kids, tell him to get rid of the old guys, because they're ahead of the kids.'"

Watters was part of one of the biggest trades in Leafs history when the team landed Mats Sundin during the NHL draft on June 28, 1994. Actually, Watters played a major role in the deal because the principals, Fletcher and Quebec Nordiques GM Pierre Lacroix, were not on speaking terms.

"This went back to when Lacroix was still an agent," Watters said. "When Vincent Damphousse got traded from the Leafs to the Edmonton Oilers for Grant Fuhr, his agent was Pierre Lacroix. He and

Cliff had a falling out because they had a [contract] worked out for the Leafs and Cliff shipped him to Edmonton without completing it. From that point on, Pierre was not interested in talking to Cliff.

"When Pierre took over the Nordiques, he called me at the end of May and said, 'Hey Willie, we got to make a deal. I'll give you Sundin, you give me Clark and Lefebvre.' I said, 'That's a lot. We've got to get something back for that.' So Lacroix said we'll leave it until the draft."

Lacroix had a lot of talent on the Nordiques, but he felt Clark would add the toughness his team lacked. Sylvain Lefebvre was a dependable stay-at-home defenceman who was also sought by Los Angeles Kings GM Sam McMaster.

"The draft was in Hartford, and we were talking to Sam McMaster," Watters said. "He wanted Lefebvre and was willing to trade his number-one pick to let us move up in the draft. Cliff really wanted Brett Lindros. He thought if he could get L.A.'s pick at seven [overall], he could get Brett Lindros.

"Now we were at the stage where I told Cliff, 'We better go back to Lacroix because if we can get Sundin, we got to tell [McMaster]. It was the day before the draft, and I said, 'Pierre, if we make a deal, we've got to make it now, because we've got a deal on the table for Lefebvre.' So we proceeded to make the deal. Nobody knew about that deal until the next day when it was announced at the draft."

The trade was Mats Sundin and fellow forward Todd Warriner, defenceman Garth Butcher, and Quebec's first-round draft pick in 1994 (later traded to the Washington Capitals) to the Leafs for Clark, Lefebvre, forward Landon Wilson, and the Leafs' first-round pick.

The deal was not concluded, however, until a long and painful session with the Nordiques' notoriously cheap managing partner, Marcel Aubut, to finalize the financial arrangements.

"That was akin to Chinese water torture," Watters said. "This guy tried to get everything out of you. There was money owing on the Michel Petit contract from when he came from Nordiques to the Leafs [four years earlier] that he wanted to wipe off. We finally announced the deal, but Cliff was in for another hour and a half with Aubut, trying to finalize all the ramifications.

"But through it all, I don't think Cliff ever talked to Pierre. That made it an interesting deal, but I don't think we would have made it had Sam McMaster not wanted Lefebvre."

One of Watters' worst nights as assistant GM was on March 4, 1996, when Pat Burns was fired as head coach. GM Cliff Fletcher decided both the coach and the team needed a change. But the Leafs tried to keep it quiet until an official announcement the next day. The news leaked out, however, through Burns' cousin Robin, who was his agent, and a security guard at Maple Leaf Gardens who stumbled across a farewell message to the players written on a board in the dressing room. The security guard called the *Toronto Sun* late that night, and the cat was out of the bag.

The end came for Burns after a loss the previous night in Denver to the Colorado Avalanche. Fletcher delivered the news the next day at the team hotel, shortly before the Leafs flew home to Toronto. By that night, the rumours were all over the city.

Watters, who was still trying to keep the news quiet, was caught in the crossfire, some of which was coming from yours truly, because Fletcher was not answering his telephone.

"Burns had signed his new contract in January, but from the point he signed it, he was never happy in Toronto," Watters said. "At least, that was my perception. We went to Colorado, and Burnsie said, 'Willie, when are you going to fire me?' I said, 'I'm not going to fire you, we gotta win. Let's go.'

"Cliff finally saw that we had to make a change. So we decided what we were going to do. We lost to Colorado on Sunday night. Monday morning, we were all heading back to Toronto. I got a call in the morning about eight o'clock. It was Burnsie. He said, 'What's going on? When are you going to fire me? I said, 'I'm not going to fire you.' He said, 'It's hopeless. They're not playing for me.'

"So I called Cliff and said, 'If you're going to fire him, now is the time. Cliff went up to Burns' room, and I don't consider it a firing—it's a releasing. Then we went to the airport for the flight home.

"After we were in the air, Cliff said, 'We let him go. We're going to hire Nick [Beverley]. Nick had come in from a scouting assignment on Sunday night, and we talked to him about it. Then everybody was sworn to secrecy.

"We did not say anything on Monday. We were going to announce it Tuesday. Nobody was supposed to know about it. We were all in business class on the plane. Burnsie was here, I was behind him.

"Burns leaned around the seat and said to me something about Cliff saying 'You wanted me fired.' I said, 'Burnsie, get lost.' The rest of the guys didn't know he'd been fired—just Cliff, Bob Stellick, and me. So at the Toronto airport I said, 'Bye, Burnsie, good luck.'"

Watters went home. At the time, Fletcher's marriage had ended, and he was in a new relationship. He did not want to be reached by anyone, so when news about Burns started to leak out, everyone called Watters.

"I start fielding calls," Watters said. "I said he'd not been fired, because at that point it was not official. Little did I know there had been a call to RDS [a French-language sports network] saying he resigned. There was no resignation, so then I said he hadn't resigned.

"Then Damien Cox [of the *Toronto Star*] called me. I said, 'I can't say anything. We have a meeting in morning.' I told you the same, I told Scott [Morrison of the *Toronto Sun*] the same thing."

The problem was, Burns left town right after he got off the plane. He picked up a few clothes, stopped at the Gardens, and left a farewell message to the players, then hopped in his truck to drive to Montreal. Not long after that, RDS reported Burns had quit, and the media frenzy was on.

"We couldn't find Cliff," Watters said. "Bob [Stellick] called and said, 'What do we do?' I said, 'We do what Cliff told us to do. This is highly secretive shit.'

"Then you called again, Damien called again, everybody called again. I still said Burns had not resigned. Then Scotty Morrison called back at midnight. He said, 'We have it from the security guard.' I said,

'You've got to do what you've got to do.' We had no authority to release it.

"Cliff finally called about 12:30 and said, 'What's going on?' I said, 'What's going on!'

"'Oh, shit,' Cliff said. Burnsie hung us out to dry.

"The next day, you and a bunch of other people were mad at me. That was a story that bothered me, because I had to manipulate the truth. That was not my style."

6

McGILL'S MEMORIES

Bob McGill is from the long line of tough Western Canadian boys who found a home with the Toronto Maple Leafs. He joined the Leafs in 1981 at 19 years of age, one of a trio of teenage defencemen—Jim Benning and Fred Boimistruck were the others—rushed into service. McGill was considered the least talented of the three, but he managed to have the best NHL career thanks to a solid work ethic and a willingness to drop his gloves when necessary. Benning and Boimistruck were out of the NHL relatively quickly, done in by great expectations from a bad team that did not allow them any time to develop. McGill managed to get in a couple of learning stints in the minor leagues after his first season with the Leafs. By the end of his career in 1994, after stops in Toronto, Chicago, San Jose, Detroit, Toronto again, New York and finally Hartford, McGill was a dependable stay-at-home defenceman.

He now lives in Newmarket, Ontario, near Toronto and does some broadcasting for Leafs TV and radio.

When McGill was brought up to the Leafs in 1981, he was excited to be in the NHL, but even he could see it was a mistake. Defence is the hardest position to learn, and expecting three teenagers to learn it at the NHL level was sheer folly.

"I was 19, Jim Benning was 18, and Fred Boimistruck was 19," McGill said. "I could see maybe having two of us up there when you look back on it. There was a story in *The Hockey News* that year, called 'The Good, The Bad and The Gifted.'

"The good was Freddy, the gifted was Jimmy, and the bad was me, because I was the bad-boy tough guy. We weren't a very good team, and to put three young defencemen on a team like that wasn't very good. It threw you right in the fire."

Benning, who was drafted sixth overall by the Leafs in 1981, managed to play 605 NHL games for the Leafs and Vancouver Canucks, but he never lived up to his promise. Boimistruck played 83 games for the Leafs over two seasons and then, after a few seasons in the minor leagues, was out of hockey by 1987. He is now a train engineer in Northwestern Ontario.

Another supremely talented young defenceman joined the Maple Leafs during McGill's tenure. Al (Alfie) Iafrate could skate hard. He was big and had a tremendous slapshot. But his personality was a lot different than the average hockey player's. McGill fondly remembers him as one of the most memorable characters he ever played with.

"Back in those days, a lot of players smoked," McGill said. "Alfie was one of the worst for that. I can remember rooming with him, and you'd wake up in the middle of the night and you'd smell cigarette smoke. You'd turn over and see a bright red cherry going on the other bed. He'd be up smoking.

"Al was a great guy, but he danced to his own drum. He was a funny guy. In the morning, you'd wake up, and on the nightstand you'd see about ten cigarettes. They would all be upside down and burned right down to the filter. He would light one off the other one, set it upside down, and all you'd see in the morning was the filter standing up, burned right down."

Later in his career, Iafrate began to lose his hair and he became quite sensitive about it. This was in the late 1980s, before baldness became fashionable, and Iafrate preferred to hide his growing bald spot under his hockey helmet. As the best defenceman on the team, Iafrate was usually one of the starting pair, which meant he had to stand on the blueline in front of the crowd with his helmet off for the national anthems. He hated that.

McGill remembers Iafrate's complex about his hair had his teammates roaring with laughter on the bench at Madison Square Garden during a game against the New York Rangers.

"This was probably the funniest thing I ever saw in hockey," McGill said. "Al was coming up the ice about 100 miles an hour. He tried to go around Tom Laidlaw [of the Rangers] and he hip-checked him. Al slid along the top of the boards and slammed into the glass. It stopped him dead.

The glass that goes around the boards at the Garden stops at the end of each players' bench. That edge of the glass is wrapped in padding, but every once in a while a player would get run into it and knocked cold.

"He hit the glass, his helmet went flying, and he was laying on the ice in front of the bench. His helmet wound up about 15 feet away. We all thought he was dead.

"All of a sudden, he started to move but he was crawling on his belly, just using his arms. Everyone said, 'Look, he's going for his helmet.' Sure enough, he pulled himself all the way to his helmet. He put it on his head and then rolled over and just lay there.

"Well, the guys on the bench were almost peeing themselves laughing. You could see the whole thing unfolding."

On another occasion, a line brawl broke out during a Leafs game. Iafrate joined the fray, and his helmet came off at one point. He suddenly disappeared and was next spotted crawling among the legs, gloves, and sticks on the ice. Iafrate worked his way through the crowd until he located his helmet. He plopped it back on his head, stood up, found another dance partner, and resumed fighting.

Iafrate was not one to spend much time in the gym. He figured his natural gifts as a player were enough. For his sophomore season in the

NHL, Iafrate showed up for training camp well above his playing weight. The media dubbed him Al I-a-fatty. McGill says coaches Dan Maloney and John Brophy took drastic action. They decreed extra sessions of bag skating, where players have to do skating drills to the point of exhaustion, plus much more.

"He showed up, 19 years old and 238 pounds," McGill said. "He didn't do anything all summer. He still had a washboard stomach at 238, but his legs and his butt were so big it was scary.

"He could still skate, but he would go twice around the ice and he was dead. Maloney and Brophy almost killed him at training camp. He would get bagged big time after every skate, and that was when we used to have two-a-days.

"Then at end of the day, when everybody else got to go home, they would take him downstairs under the Hot Stove Lounge. They had an exercise bike in the sauna in the basement. He was allowed only to take his skates and gloves off. He had his full equipment on, riding the exercise bike in the sauna.

"They sat him out of all the preseason games until the end, and then they let him play the final exhibition game in Buffalo. Iafrate ended up in a fight with Sean McKenna. McKenna was a lefty and tagged him and broke his cheekbone and his nose.

"Al was in the hospital for ten days because he had surgery on his nose and cheekbone and couldn't eat solid food. It was the best thing that ever happened to him. He lost all the weight and came out of the hospital at 218."

John Brophy was known for his fiery relationships with his players. As a hard-working, tough player, though, McGill developed a good rapport with the coach.

"I never had any problems with coaches because I worked hard in

Like his predecessor Ian Turnbull, Leaf defenceman Al Iafrate lived life on his terms.

practice," McGill said. "Broph was a guy where, away from the rink, he was an awesome guy. He had so much intensity. He was one of those coaches who yelled all the time. He yelled and screamed, yelled and screamed, and after a while, guys just tuned him out.

"But he used to have some of the best one-liners ever. I'll never forget one night when we were in Minnesota. We were down 4–1 after the first period at the Met Center, and he came in and started yelling at the guys.

"He said to Todd Gill, 'You've got as much intensity right now as my fucking dick, and that's none.' The guys were bending over, holding their mouths shut.

"And he would always talk about St. Catharines, because it was our farm team. He'd say, 'Steve Thomas, you want to go to St. Catharines? It's only 70 miles there, but it's seven thousand miles back.'"

Brophy had his own way of doing things, which usually involved hard work. Many of the players on other teams in the NHL found his methods outdated, a point McGill conceded. But, he says, those qualities made him a great minor-league coach. After he was fired by the Leafs, Brophy went to the East Coast Hockey League, a few rungs down the hockey ladder, and had a long run of success.

"Broph was an old-school guy," McGill said. "Teams used to watch us in our pregame skates and laugh. They used to say, 'What are you guys doing?' Our morning skates were tougher than a lot of teams' practices. You'd wonder why you would come out and have no legs in the games sometimes. He'd have us skating down-and-backs.

"He didn't know the word *preparation* as in 'light skate, work on a few things.' He'd say, 'You come to the rink, you work, work, work. The way he played the game, he was an intimidator, and that's the way he coached. That is why he was always successful at the minor-league level. He could intimidate the young guys. 'You had better work, or you will be out of here.'

"But a lot of guys who played for him loved him because away from the rink he was a great guy. It's amazing when you talk to kids who played in the East Coast league for Broph and made the NHL. They say he taught them about work ethic. You take that with you."

Brad Smith, aka Motor City Smitty, was another of the memorable characters that McGill played with in Toronto. McGill, and a couple other of our storytellers, say Smitty's best caper was Herb Tarlek Day, named after the smarmy ad salesman on the television show *WKRP in Cincinnati*. Herb favoured loud suits with a white belt and shoes to match.

"We played in Winnipeg, and we were staying overnight and flying to L.A. the next day, so a couple of weeks in advance we decided we were having a Herb Tarlek Day," McGill said. "It was Motor City Smitty who organized it. You had to bring the loudest clothes you could find and put them on. Then you had to check out of the hotel, get on the bus, go through the airport in Winnipeg, fly to Vancouver, get off the plane, go through customs in Vancouver, get back on the plane, fly to L.A., get your luggage, go to the hotel and check in. Then you could take your Tarlek clothes off.

"I went to the Sally Ann [Salvation Army store] and bought a polyester sports coat in a wild colour, and I had a freaking tie that was this wide. Chris Kotsopoulos had the best outfit. He went through his old man's closet and got these red polyester pants and white dress shoes.

"It was funny because guys would say to [head coach] Dan Maloney, 'You just went to your closet and got a suit from when you played.' It was a lot of fun and one of the funniest things we ever did.

"We won in Winnipeg. It was a Sunday night and nothing was open, so guys just hung out in the hotel and emptied their mini-bars. We got up in the morning still feeling good about ourselves because we were going into L.A. a couple days ahead of the game.

7

HEALY AND THE LATTER-DAY LEAFS

Glenn Healy was an NHL goaltender for 14 years, the last four with the Toronto Maple Leafs from 1997 to 2001. He was not an eccentric in a position known for its oddballs, but he can lay claim to being the funniest goaltender in NHL history.

When the Toronto Maple Leafs beat the Montreal Canadiens 3–2 in the first game at the brand-new Air Canada Centre in February 1999, Healy said, "Best game we ever played here. You could look it up, but I don't think we've ever lost to those guys here."

It is also quite likely that Healy is the only goalie in NHL history to play the bagpipes. He marched and played with the 48th Highlanders in the parade that opened the Air Canada Centre and celebrates his Scottish heritage by piping between television appearances for TSN.

Healy and tough guy Tie Domi finished their careers with the Maple Leafs, but both played together on the New York Rangers earlier in the 1990s. One night in a bar in Chicago, Healy had a first-hand look at how tough Domi was when Ranger teammate Paul Broten ran into some unfriendly customers.

"A group of guys were picking on Paul Broten," Healy said. "Tie made his way over and said, 'What's the problem?' One of the guys said, 'None of your business, you midget.' So Tie said it is now.

"He picked the biggest guy and said, 'All right, you get the first shot.' The guy said, 'I'm not going to hit you.' Tie said, 'If you don't hit me, I'll hit you. So I'll give you the first shot.'

"So the guy reached back with a right hand and threw a big punch. Tie put his head down and the guy cracked him right on the thickest part of Tie's head. Tie looked up and said, 'That couldn't be your best shot. I'll give you one more.' But the guy couldn't throw another right because he'd cracked his knuckles on Tie's head. So he threw a left and that didn't do anything, either.

"Tie said, 'Now it's my turn.' He must have hit him 75 times, and that would be on the light side."

Domi took his role as Leaf enforcer very seriously, to Healy's chagrin on one occasion.

"We were playing in Jersey, and I was the backup goalie like I was most nights with Curtis Joseph," Healy said. "I was sitting on the bench and [New Jersey Devils forward] Krzysztof Oliwa was standing by the bench. We were just having some small talk. Well, Tie was infuriated that anyone would talk to our bench.

"We were actually just having a conversation, but Tie stepped on the ice and knocked him out. I felt somewhat guilty about that. 'And how's your family Krzysztof?' Wham! 'Thanks for coming.'"

On the first day of every training camp, a group of students from York University would help conduct fitness tests on the Maple Leafs players. Domi was always proud of his fitness level, proud enough to take a dim view of anyone who thought otherwise.

"The students were always pretty eager to test the guys because this was a real learning experience for them to see that level of athlete,"

Glenn Healy kept them laughing as a Leaf goalie.

Healy said. "But one guy came to regret doing the sit-up test. The rule was that if your feet came off the floor while you were doing the sit-up, the test was over.

"Tie got his second warning, and the student stopped Tie when his feet came up for the third time. But Tie thought he still had at least 20 more sit-ups in the tank and started to throttle the kid. I don't think the kid ever saw a sit-up test like that."

Ken (Bomber) Baumgartner and Tie Domi were both good NHL fighters and were teammates briefly on the Leafs in the mid-1990s. Healy played with Baumgartner on the Los Angeles Kings early in his career, then became Domi's teammate on the New York Rangers. Healy says the most entertaining fight he ever saw was between Domi and Baumgartner at Madison Square Garden. The entertainment came from the action after the fight, when Baumgarter poked fun at the size of Domi's head.

"After the fight was over, Ken picked up Tie's helmet and spun it on his head like a top," Healy said. "That helmet was like a cradle, it was so big. The crowd thought that was quite funny.

"While he was in the penalty box, Tie got a white towel and some scissors. He cut the towel in strips. Back then, Bomber had the long, blonde locks. Just before he went back on the ice, Tie put the towel on his head. As he made his way back to the bench, he fluffed his fingers through the strips like they were Bomber's hair. The whole Garden just went nuts."

After Domi was traded to Toronto, Leaf captain Doug Gilmour had an annual gag about the size of his noggin. Every year at Halloween, Gilmour would bring a pumpkin into the Leaf dressing room and draw a face on it. Then he would steal Domi's helmet, put it on the

Tie Domi knew how to fight and how to get laughs.

pumpkin and put it in Domi's locker just before the media came into the room.

Healy's pointed sense of humour often put him at odds with his coaches, from Pat Quinn in Toronto to Mike Keenan in New York. His relationship with Keenan was especially fractious. Healy remembers two incidents that erased any chance they would ever get along.

One happened the day before the NHL's trade deadline, when the Rangers were flying to Calgary. Healy had a large contract from his days with the New York Islanders, but after he was traded to the Rangers, he was the backup goalie. The contract meant Healy was a prime candidate to be traded on deadline day.

"The day before the trade deadline, Keenan came up to me on the flight," Healy said. "I was beside [Rangers GM] Neil Smith. Keenan said, 'Now that you're both here together, we're going to get you on the same page.' I was wondering what was going on and thought, 'Oh, oh, these guys set this up because it's the day before trade deadline.'

"Keenan said, 'Neil, did you tell Glenn he was going to play every single game?'

"'Of course not.'

"'Now Glenn, did Neil tell you you were going to play every game?'

"'No, of course not.'

Then Keenan said, 'You're not playing. What concerns you?' I said, 'You've got to be kidding.'

"I was making an exorbitant amount of money, so I told him I wasn't a hooker, he couldn't pay me all that money to screw me.

"He didn't like that line at all. That was when we headed for divorce."

The clincher, Healy said, came after he shut out the Washington Capitals just before Christmas one year. It came to a head when Healy was talking to a reporter and mentioned his coach with the New York

Islanders, Al Arbour, who guided the Isles to four consecutive Stanley Cups in the early 1980s.

"We used to have these segment bonuses where you would get so much money if you got through five games," Healy said. "If you won so many games, if your penalty killing was so good, your power play was so good, your goals-against, and so on, you would get paid bonus money. You could get as much as $5,000 for a five-game segment.

"So we beat the Capitals 1–0. We hit our penalty-killing bonus, goals-against bonus, our wins bonus, and it was a power-play goal by Adam Graves, so we hit everything. This meant thousands of dollars two days before Christmas.

"Our next game was on December 27, and we were playing New Jersey. A reporter asked me after the Washington game if I was going to play against New Jersey because I got a shutout. I said, 'I can't figure this guy out. If it was Al Arbour, I could tell you if I was playing, but I don't know.'

"The next day, the headline in the newspaper said, Keenan: No Al Arbour. Keenan was not happy. He called me into his office. He called me Mr. Fucking-Know-It-All and Gordie Howe about 15 times. Then he said, 'What's the difference between me and Al Arbour?'

"So I said, 'Four Cups.'

"I think we officially broke up that day. We were done."

During the 2000-01 season, the Leafs and their fans were preoccupied with the chances of getting Eric Lindros in a trade with the Philadelphia Flyers. In the end, it was clear Flyers GM Bobby Clarke had no intention of trading Lindros, who still had star value, to his hometown team. But for weeks leading up to the trade deadline in March, there were mood swings in everyone from the fans to head coach and GM Pat Quinn depending on the trade talks.

"You could always tell where the negotiations were by Pat Quinn's speeches," Healy said. "If he was real close to getting Lindros, and he thought he was going to close the deal, he'd come in and tell us we were all crap. He'd say, 'I'll get fucking players in here who fucking want to play, and I'll show you.'

"Curtis [Joseph] and I used to look at each other and say, 'He's coming, we can tell.' Then, when the deal started to go sour, the speeches would always turn to, 'We're all in this together. All for one, one for all. Don't let the guy beside you down.'

"Then the next day, Bobby Clarke would have a moment of weakness and we'd be back to crap again. 'I'll get rid of all of you guys if I have to,' Quinn would say. This went on for months."

When the big-money era for the players came along in the early 1990s, they began looking after themselves more and drinking less to maximize their earning years. But saloons, the traditional postgame playgrounds for players, never went out of fashion, nor did every player take a vow of abstinence.

Healy says he was not present for this story, although it was firmly a part of Leaf legend by the time he arrived in Toronto.

"There was the time in Vancouver that a couple of the Russian players got cut off at last call," he said. "The next thing you know, a bottle was hurled through the air and hit the bartender. He was cut for a couple of stitches.

"The next day the people at the bar demanded an apology from the Leafs. They were like, hold on, it was a crowded bar, how do you know it was us? The people from the bar said, well, the guy who did it was Russian.

"So the Leafs asked what kind of beer bottle hit the bartender. Heineken. Right away the Leafs said, 'Okay, we'll get an apology for you.' They knew they had a Russian player who loved to throw back about a thousand Heinekens."

Healy is a native of Pickering, Ontario, a bedroom community of Toronto. He bought a house on Lake Ontario near his hometown, and after he wound up with the Leafs in 1997, he often had his new teammates over for parties.

"Just after we moved there, I had a team party, and Felix Potvin decided to burn all my patio furniture," Healy said. "He decided there wasn't enough firewood. At the same time as all my furniture was burning, Kris King put on my kilt and all my bag-pipe stuff and made his way down to the fire pit in my feather bonnet. That was significantly more expensive than my patio furniture.

"King had disappeared, and all of a sudden I heard this distant sound of awful bag-piping. He was dressed for battle, he was ready to go.

"I had just moved in, too, and I could see all my neighbours looking out their windows. I know they were all thinking, 'There goes the neighbourhood.'"

A more memorable bash came at the end of the 1998-99 season when the team went for a round of golf followed by dinner at a steakhouse in downtown Toronto.

"We lost to Buffalo [in the Stanley Cup semifinals] and we were playing some golf," Healy said. "Well, most of us were playing golf. The Russian players were playing bumper cars with the golf carts, which is what they liked to do.

"We went from there to Ruth's Chris. We had this private room in the back where we had our steaks. I arranged to get a pipe band to come in and play. So Kris King held one door, I held the other, and 32 players in this pipe band marched in right through the restaurant. The people in the restaurant were wondering what was going on. One after another, in came the band, and they played their set in the back room.

"We were having a good old time. Danny Markov was doing his Russian Cossack dance and Tie Domi decided to have a little fun, so he was dancing, too. Markov decided to finish his dance by throwing a shot glass. Well, Tie was about 80 feet away from him, but didn't Markov hit him right on the head. He couldn't have hit him again if he tried, although it was a big target.

"Now the performance was over and the race was on. Domi chased him out of the room, through the restaurant and out the doors."

8

THE BURKE YEARS

Officially, the Brian Burke era began November 29, 2008, when he was named the Maple Leafs' 13th general manager. But it really began several months earlier when he quickly emerged as the search committee's top and practically only candidate. This set off a long, slow dance as the Leafs and Burke waited for his present employer, the Anaheim Ducks, to finally grant permission for him to walk away from his contract.

Cliff Fletcher, who brought the Leafs back to respectability in the early 1990s when he replaced Floyd Smith as GM, agreed to serve as interim general manager when John Ferguson was fired in January, 2008. Five months later, it became obvious that Burke was the GM-in-waiting when Fletcher hired his great friend Ron Wilson as head coach.

Wilson and Burke became friends when they were teammates in the mid-1970s on the Providence College hockey team. Wilson was the star forward, the product of an NHL family—his father Larry and uncle Johnny both played and coached in the league—while Burke was the product of a working-class Irish family with a rough-and-tumble playing style to match.

The legendary Lou Lamoriello ran the Providence hockey program for many years before he went on to make his mark in the NHL as GM of the New Jersey Devils. He was and still is Burke's most important mentor in all areas of his life. Burke says it was Lamoriello who pointed him in the direction of law school when it was clear his playing career was not headed toward the NHL. Burke did stick with hockey long enough to sign a contract with the Philadelphia Flyers and play one season in the American Hockey League; but he graduated from Harvard Law School in 1981 and started his route to the NHL on the managerial side.

Unlike a lot of the other periods in Leaf history, even the ones marked by little other than losing, there have not been a lot of laughs in the Burke era. This is only partly the fault of Burke, who is gruff and can be quick to anger, and Wilson, a caustic sort whose smart-alec persona and sense of humor can come across as condescending. And the Burke era is defined by those two, as new head coach Randy Carlyle has not been around long enough to establish a presence, and the current crop of players, perhaps because they're so young, does not have any dominant personalities.

The real trouble is the media glare on the Maple Leafs, always intense in Canada's most densely-populated region, became white-hot with the advent of bloggers, social media and 24/7 coverage from two sports television networks, two sports radio stations, four daily newspapers, all of the other web sites and TV and radio stations, not to mention the team's own television outlet. Coupled with the fans' anger over Burke's inability to quickly correct Ferguson's mistakes and turn the Leafs into a winner, the relentless coverage created a toxic mix that often left Burke and Wilson ill-tempered.

While Burke's blowups with the media can be louder than Wilson's, his relationship with reporters is generally better than his head coach's. Wilson's sarcastic humour often created more hard feelings than he may have intended with reporters; but his tendency to use the media as a scapegoat for the troubles of his team by exaggerating (at best) some of their pronouncements did not win him many friends.

Wilson's attitude toward the media is best described by an incident at Madison Square Garden after the Leafs lost a tough game to the New York Rangers. When Wilson appeared for his post-game scrum there was the usual crush of media thanks to the convergence of the New York crowd and the mob that follows the Leafs around these days.

The crowd was so large that Stan Fischler, a veteran New York hockey writer who also works the television broadcasts, got to the front of the pack by kneeling down and practically crawling to Wilson's feet. As Fischler held his microphone up to Wilson, the coach looked down and cackled.

"It's about time you got down on your knees to ask me questions," Wilson said. "They should be doing that in Toronto, but they don't."

As Kevin McGran of the *Toronto Star* tells it, Wilson also let the Toronto media folks know his feelings when the Leafs paid a visit to his former team, the San Jose Sharks. It was the first time Wilson and the Leafs went to San Jose after the Sharks fired him at the end of the 2007-08 season.

Following the Leafs' morning skate on the day of the game, Wilson was talking to the Toronto media when David Pollak, who covers the Sharks for the *San Jose Mercury News*, walked by with a colleague. Wilson pointed to the San Jose reporters and said, "The San Jose guys ask more intelligent questions than you guys."

A few minutes later, McGran and a couple of other Toronto reporters were chatting with Pollak about Wilson's remark. Pollak said, "In the whole time Wilson was here, that's the most he's ever said about us in a positive vein."

Another visit to San Jose resulted in a career milestone for Wilson followed by a run-in with the NHL head office caused by his favourite whipping boys, the media. The Leafs played the Sharks on January 11, 2011, and Wilson was looking for his 600th win as an NHL head coach. At the time, he was the leader among active NHL coaches in wins.

It is customary in the NHL for players and coaches to offer cash to their teammates and players for a win against a former team. While the players realize the significance of such games and usually put out a little extra effort, even if the beneficiary is not universally admired, the money is appreciated, too. If a win results, it usually goes toward a night on the town for the whole team. Only those who have not seen players fight tooth-and-nail over a penny-ante card game would be surprised how a few hundred bucks can motivate a room full of millionaires.

Leafs defenceman Carl Gunnarsson, who was too young and inexperienced to realize the significance of what he was doing, spilled the beans. After the game-day skate, he mentioned to the Toronto media that Wilson pinned $600 to the bulletin board in the dressing room as an obvious incentive for his 600th win.

Naturally, when the Leafs beat the Sharks 4-2 to get Wilson his milestone, all of the stories and reports played up the angle of the coach offering the cash to his players. It all seemed like harmless fun until the humourless beancounters at NHL headquarters in New York got wind of it. In their eyes, it may have been only $600 but it was a violation of the collective agreement as it pertains to the salary cap. Really.

Ever since the cap was introduced after the lockout wiped out the 2004-05 season, the league keeps an eagle eye out for possible circumvention of the player salary limits. Thus any exchange of cash on the side between players and management is strictly forbidden. When the NHL bosses found out about the $600, Wilson and the Leafs were fined. The amount was not disclosed but it's safe to say it was far in excess of six hundred bucks.

"No comment, period," Wilson said after the NHL cracked down.

There was much comment by the fans on Twitter, Facebook and other forms of media after Wilson was nailed by the league. It may have been the most sympathy he received from Leafs Nation during his turbulent reign as the the team's head coach. There was also a lot of head-shaking in dressing rooms around the rest of the NHL.

The Leafs moved on to Phoenix after the Sharks win and Lance Hornby of the *Toronto Sun* tells us the topic was the subject of discussion among the Phoenix Coyotes. But Coyotes head coach Dave Tippett wanted no part of it when he was asked if he happened to wave around some cabbage when he took the Coyotes into Dallas the first time after he was fired by the Stars and they got Tippett the win.

"No comment, but we did win and I had to buy lunch, for the coaches, not the players," Tippett said. "I guess rules are rules. They're written a certain way and you have to abide by them. "Maybe things like that should be left in the dressing room and then no one has to worry about it. It's an inconsequential thing that happens time and again with players and now and then with coaches." Coyotes captain Shane Doan was not so reticent. He complimented Wilson for the touch of putting up $600 for win number 600 ("That's thinking on your feet.") and then employed some sarcasm worthy of the coach himself.

"I've never, ever heard anything about anyone putting any money up on any board," Doan said. "I'm sure that's the first time."

Hornby, who has seen his share of Leafs coaches come and go in his three decades on the beat, discovered a softer side to Wilson when he heard about a favour done for the coach by the team's television producer and the game's leading archivist.

Wilson's father Larry died in 1979 of a heart attack at the age of 49, and Ron always regretted that he never got to see his father play in the NHL. While the elder Wilson had a long career in the American Hockey League with the Buffalo Bisons, he only played 156 NHL games, with the last one coming in 1955 not long after Ron was born. The coach happened to mention this to Leafs TV producer Mark Askin and he decided to see if he could make it happen with the help of Paul Patskou, who is famous to those in the sports television business for finding rare pieces of hockey film.

Patskou went to Canada's National Archives and searched for films of games between the Maple Leafs and the Chicago Blackhawks from Larry Wilson's two biggest NHL seasons, 1953-54 and 1954-55, when he was a regular with the Blackhawks. While the Leafs were a staple on the Saturday night "Hockey Night In Canada" telecasts of the day, not every game was preserved on film. But Patskou found a 16mm film of a Leaf-Blackhawks game from the 1954-55. season. A check of the game summary showed Larry Wilson was not only in the lineup but scored a goal.

The coach told Hornby it was an emotional experience watching his late father as a young man.

"It was really neat to watch him at age 24," Wilson said. "He looks exactly like the next brother to me, Brad, about 5-foot-8, or 5-9. The cool thing is the date, November 6th, 1954, and my Mom's pregnant with me.

"He scores a goal and has a penalty and a significant role in the game. I remember he was a good skater, but when he was 34 or 35, I'd seen him on the downside. But to see him compete like that. . . ."

Larry Wilson scored his goal late in the 5-2 win by the Leafs and Wilson realized there was another connection in that game.

"When I got [the game] on my iPad I called in Dave Morrison, our head of amateur scouting, whose dad Jimmy played for the Leafs," Wilson said. "I knew all the players in the game and told him: 'Watch this, you're not going to believe it.' So he sees my dad score on a pass from Bill Mosienko and on the next faceoff, Jimmy goes down and scores for Toronto. George Armstrong scored first, my dad ties it up, Jimmy scores . . . it's amazing all the people I know while watching it. Really cool."

The game also showed Wilson the great differences between the way hockey was played in the 1950s and 1960s and today's fast-and-furious version when players hit the ice for a maximum of 40 seconds a shift but spend all of it at top speed.

"The players take three-minute shifts. You can't believe it," Wilson said. "My dad doesn't get out for the first seven minutes because everyone else takes a long shift. And there's nothing but turnovers. To watch that game now, you're going: 'Holy crap, what's going on?' But it's a full game. You can watch him taking faceoffs, the whole nine yards. It was great."

With a few exceptions, Brian Burke does not carry grudges for a lifetime, although he does not forget them quickly, either, as *Toronto Star* hockey writer Kevin McGran discovered on a visit with the Leafs to Boston on St. Patrick's Day in 2012.

Back in November 2011, McGran had written a story that noted the Leafs, for the first time in their 85-year history, did not have a player on the roster from the Greater Toronto Area. In fact, since they sent down prospect Nazem Kadri, who hails from London, Ontario, two hours to the west, the Leafs did not even have a player from Ontario. Given the number of NHL players who come from the GTA, which has a population of about five million, this was rather unusual.

While the story quoted an official from the Greater Toronto Hockey League, the biggest and best children's circuit in the province, saying this provided no encouragement for local youngsters to shoot for the Maple Leafs, McGran didn't think of his story as an indictment of Burke's recruiting. He just thought it was an anomaly worth noting.

Burke, though, thought otherwise. The topic was a sensitive one because Burke is an American (although he actually holds dual citizenship from his days as GM of the Vancouver Canucks) and Wilson, although he was born in Canada, is also a U.S. citizen. Prior to McGran's story, the proud Canadian Don Cherry, the most famous broadcaster and Leaf fan in hockey, took regular potshots at Burke for, in his view, signing too many Americans and Europeans.

The day the story came out, McGran was in Montreal where the Leafs were about to play the Canadiens. He went to the Bell Centre and ran into Burke, who looked away when he saw him.

"I asked, 'Are you mad at me?'" McGran said. "He said, 'Damn right I am.' He thought I wrote it with the express purpose of making him look bad. I said, 'No, I was just pointing out a historical fact.'

"But he wouldn't talk to me for three weeks."

By March, when McGran was in Boston on St. Patrick's Day ahead of the Leafs game, he thought Burke was over his pique. At least he did until he went to the Leafs hotel. He ran into Leafs executive Dave Poulin, who invited McGran to join him and Patrick Burke, Brian's oldest son who is a scout for the Philadelphia Flyers, for a drink in the lobby bar.

Poulin told McGran that the seat he was offered had been occupied by

Brian Burke, who had just left for his room. McGran didn't think much of it and sat down and chatted with Poulin and the younger Burke for about 45 minutes.

Then he saw Brian Burke come back into the bar. Burke took one look at McGran sitting at the table with his son and Poulin, glared at the hockey writer and pointedly sat elsewhere. The grudge was still in full bloom.

The visit with Poulin and Patrick Burke was not a loss, though. Patrick, who grew up in the Boston area with his mother, Brian Burke's first wife, and still lived there, told a tale of one of his father's visits.

First, an aside. After Burke and his first wife divorced, he vowed that he would visit his four children every second weekend no matter where he was working. He kept that promise, which cost a lot of time and money during his time as general manager of the Vancouver Canucks and Anaheim Ducks and played a role in his decision to leave Anaheim for the Toronto job.

Burke endured a lot since then, the worst being the death of his son Brendan at the age of 21 in a car accident in February 2010. But to this day, he still visits his three surviving adult children in Boston every second weekend.

On this occasion, according to Patrick, his father drove in from his off-season home in Minnesota. He and Patrick then drove to a favourite Irish pub, the Warren Tavern, in the rambunctious Irish neighbourhood of Charlestown.

After they arrived, Brian Burke started a conversation with the owner of the pub, who doubled as the bartender. Shortly after they started talking, the bartender climbed up on the bar and announced there was a mini-van with Minnesota plates parked outside and the fellow who owns it was with him.

Mystified, Burke asked the bartender why he did that.

"Because," came the reply, "if I didn't, it wouldn't be there much longer."

Of all the changes your correspondent's tired old eyes (to quote the late, great Toronto sports-writing legend Jim Hunt) have seen on the hockey beat over the years, none have had a greater impact on our jobs than the explosion of social media. Thanks to Facebook and, more importantly, Twitter, the mainstream media, as those from the blogosphere like to call us holdovers, have never seen more direct or quicker interaction between reporters, fans, players, coaches, GMs and hockey people of all description. You simply have to have a Twitter account these days to stay current.

This means the hockey beat can be a 24/7 job, especially if you cover a team that embraces Twitter. And Ron Wilson was a coach who embraced Twitter when it suited him. But he forgot that despite the vast changes in the media, an aphorism still prevailed—the media always gets the last word.

The first time it became apparent Wilson, who used computer technology in his coaching methods from the start, was into Twitter came after the Maple Leafs beat the New York Islanders on Long Island in a game a few days before Christmas in December 2011. In fact, it was the last game before the Christmas break and the win sent the Leafs into the holiday on a nice roll that kept them in playoff position in the Eastern Conference.

At the time, the youthful Leafs showed much improvement and their fans were hopeful of seeing their first playoff series since 2004. Wilson was also riding high and couldn't resist gloating.

About two hours after the game—well after Wilson finished his post-game media conference and when the coach knew reporters were probably just finished their post-game stories and enjoying the first few minutes of their own Christmas break—he went on Twitter to bring up the possibility of a contract extension. The topic was one that came up regularly since Wilson was in the last year of his deal and had to make the playoffs to get an extension.

In his tweet, Wilson dropped a hint that Santa Claus just might have that extension under the Christmas tree because the Leafs were playing so well. More than one reporter put down his post-game beer when his BlackBerry or iPhone buzzed, read the tweet, cursed and broke out his laptop for yet another story.

But the worst came on Christmas Day. This time, Wilson officially announced his one-year contract extension early Christmas morning. It was, in today's parlance, a supreme dick move. Wilson was around the NHL long enough to know his announcement would force all those reporters he disliked to leave their families, get on the phone and their computers to confirm it and then write their stories. To top it off, he refused to answer his phone.

That is why there was little to no sympathy for Wilson when the Leafs, in the words of Burke, "fell off a cliff" in the next two months. The end came on March 2, 2012, in Montreal when the Leafs fell to 12th place in the Eastern Conference after losing 10 of their previous 11 games. It was a quick and stunning fall and Burke said he had to fire his friend to relieve him from what he saw as overwhelming negativity from the fans.

Rob Longley of the *Toronto Sun* spoke for all of his peers when he tweeted about the Leafs' long slide a few days before Wilson was fired. Longley brought up Wilson announcing his own contract extension and tweeted, "Hey Ronnie, how's that going?"